Opposing the Money Lenders -

The Struggle to Abolish

Interest Slavery

by
Kerry Bolton

Opposing the Money Lenders -
The Struggle to Abolish
Interest Slavery
by
Kerry Bolton

Copyright © 2016 Black House Publishing Ltd

All rights reserved. No part of this book may be reproduced in any form by any electronic or mechanical means including photocopying, recording, or information storage and retrieval without permission in writing from the publisher.

ISBN-13: 978-1-910881-13-2

Black House Publishing Ltd
Kemp House
152 City Road
London
United Kingdom
EC1V 2NX

www.blackhousepublishing.com
Email: info@blackhousepublishing.com

Opposing the Money Lenders - The Struggle to Abolish Interest Slavery

by

Kerry Bolton

Black House Publishing Ltd

Contents

Introduction	1
Arthur Nelson Field	11
Truth About The Slump	12
The Examiner	16
The Crusade	17
The New Zealand Legion	20
World War & Security Intelligence Response	21
The Post-War Legacy	22
The Next Best Thing	24
Lending Money that Does Not Exist	26
Sweden Adopts Goods Standard Money	32
John A. Lee	35
This Debt Slavery : July, 1940, Budget Speech	62
A Letter which Every New Zealander should Read	77
John Hargrave	95
Social Credit	96
Social Credit Clearly Explained	101
What Will Social Credit Do?	110
Ezra Pound	117
Social Credit	117
What is Money For?	121
Father Charles Coughlin	133
Radio Priest	134
Social Justice	135
Money Questions and Answers	142
The Operation Of An Honest Money System	154
Gottfried Feder	173
The Breaking Of Interest Slavery	173
Inner History of the Abolition of Interest-Slavery	183
Programme for the Abolition of Interest Slavery	186
Conclusion	189

Introduction

"The most hated sort [of moneymaking], and with the greatest reason, is usury, which makes a gain out of money itself, and not from the natural use of it. For money was intended to be used in exchange, but not to increase at interest. And this term Usury which means the birth of money from money, is applied to the breeding of money, because the offspring resembles the parent. Wherefore of all modes of making money this is the most unnatural."

- *Aristotle (384-322 B.C.)*

Usury Through The Ages

Aristotle's definition of usury is perhaps the most cogent ever made. Plutarch (46-127 A.D.), in his essay *"Against Running In Debt, Or Taking Up Money Upon Usury,"* described usurers as "wretched," "vulture-like," and "barbarous." Cato the Elder (234-149 B.C.) compared usury to murder. Cicero (106-43 B.C.) stated "these profits are despicable which incur the hatred of men, such as those of... lenders of money on usury."

Contemporary financial analysts Sidney Homer, who worked for Salomon Bros., and Professor Richard Sylla, in their historical study of interest rates, state that the first known law on the issue was that of Hammurabi, 1800 B.C., during first dynasty Babylonia, who set the maximum rate of interest at 33⅓% per annum "for loans of grain, repayable in kind, and at 20% per annum for loans of silver by weight." Sumerian documents, circa 3000 B.C., "show the systematic use of credit based on loans of grain by volume and loans of metal by weight. Often these loans carried interest." "As early as 5000 B.C. in the Middle East, dates, olives, figs, nuts, or seeds of grain were probably lent to serfs, poor farmers, or dependants, and an increased portion of the harvest was expected to be returned in kind." "Earliest historic rates were reported in the range of 20-50% per annum for loans of grain and metal."

Introduction

The ancient Hindu Indian civilisation established maximum rates, and regarded usurers as evil.

In 600 B.C. in Classical Greece Solon established laws on interest when excessive debt caused economic crisis. Likewise, in Rome the "Twelve Tables" of 450 B.C., establishing the foundations of Roman law, after pervasive debt was causing servitude and crisis, established a maximum interest rate of 8⅓% per annum. When Brutus tried to charge the City of Salmais 48% for a loan Cicero reminded him that the legal maximum was 12%. The interest rate was often 4%. Some Greek "loan sharks" charged 25% per annum, and even 25% per day. (Sidney Homer and Richard Sylla, *A History of Interest Rates*, Wiley, 2005).

The Old Testament Jews were prohibited from usury among themselves: "Thou shalt not lend upon usury to thy brother; usury of money; usury of victuals; usury of anything that is lent upon usury."(Deut. 23:19). Critically for history, the Jews were given a dual moral code allowing them, among much else, to charge usury to non-Jews, and this has resulted in millennia of tragedy for Jew and Gentile alike: "Unto a stranger thou mayest lend upon usury; but unto thy brother thou shalt not lend upon usury, that the Lord thy God may bless thee in all that thou settest thine hand to in the land whither thou goest to possess it." (Deut. 23:20).

Those prohibitions, as well as the general ethical and moral character of the New Testament, and the Classical heritage including the Aristotlean, inherited by the Catholic Church, established the basis for Catholic social doctrine, in which opposition to usury was a key element. In 325 A.D. the Council of Nicaea banned usury among clerics. Under Emperor Charlemagne (768–814 A.D.) the prohibition was extended to laymen. Here usury simply meant the extraction of more than what was lent. That is in accord with what Luke (6: 35) stated in saying that one should not expect back more than one gives. In 1139, the Second Lateran Council in Rome declared that usury is theft, and usurers would have to give restitution. In the 12th and 13th centuries, strategies that concealed usury were also condemned. In 1311 the Council of Vienne declared that anyone claiming usury was a heretic and should be excommunicated (Decrees: 29).

Dante (1265–1321) placed usurers in the seventh rung of Hell, where the usurer would spend eternity with a heavy bag of money around his neck: Dante wrote: "From each neck there hung an enormous purse, each marked with its own beast and its own colours like a coat of arms. On these their streaming eyes appeared to feast." (*Inferno*, Canto XVII).

However, the Church often allowed the Jews to practice usury, and people both high-born and low would become indebted to Jewish usurers, until the strain became intolerable and there would be a pogrom. Moreover, when laws against usury slackened the pretext was an adaptation of Deut. 23:20, allowing Christian lenders to charge usury on loans to non-Christians such as Muslims, who for their part were likewise forbidden usury, which the Koran calls the sin of *riba*. (Al-Baqarah, 2:275). Likewise the loophole for the Muslim lender has been that of being able to charge a "fee" for a loan, rather than interest. The Church attitude from Medieval times became inconsistent, where at some places usury remained prohibited while in other places what was instead called "interest" was permitted, and it was justified for the recovery of "losses" by the lender, such as late payment. Hence the Lombards, who like the Jews, also became identified with money-lending, would not charge "usury" but "interest" as high as 100%. Genoa became a centre of merchant banking where usury was pursued and the Church felt powerless to act.

In Medieval England personal loans could range from 52-120% a year, depending on collateral. Frederick the Fair of Austria was borrowing at 80%, while merchants in Italy could borrow at 5-10%. The Crown of Spain was paying 40% for short-term loans, while Dutch merchants could borrow at 1¼%. (Homer and Sylla).

Usury Ascendant

The Reformation ushered a revolt against the traditional moral order of Europe, and the Protestant attitude towards usury was more equivocal, Zwingli, Luther and Calvin stating that there are circumstances in which usury is acceptable. With the division of Church and State, economic theorists began to write in defence of usury as a "progressive" form of commerce, laying the basis for the amoral merchant outlook that now grips most of the world. Money-lending was defended as a "service," a concept that is of course now taken for granted by almost everyone, as argued by the French jurist Molinaeus in his 16th century *Treatise on Contracts and Usury*. A radical departure from the traditional outlook that "money should not beget money," the Church banned Molinaeus' book and forced him into exile, but his ideas spread. It is significant

Introduction

that England was the first to establish a legal rate of interest, at 10%, in 1545 under Henry VIII, given the revolt in Faith he ushered. Usury was banned seven years later. According to Homer and Sylla: " During the Reformation many Protestant leaders defended interest and credit. As a result, the usury doctrine, which had held a firm grip on Jews and Christians for 2000 years, was weakened and finally deserted." (Homer and Sylla, 77).

A century later the focus on economic thinking shifted to Holland where usury was defended as productive and essential by economic theorists such as Claudius Salmasius (1588–1653). Holland became the centre of banking, and the model for the Bank of England. English utilitarian philosophers such as Adam Smith, and Jeremy Bentham who wrote *A Defence of Usury* justified the social utility of usury. Other fathers of English economics, David Ricardo, Jean Baptiste Say, and John Stuart Mill, went further in saying that there should be no restraints on contracting parties in money-lending.

The Bank of England was founded as a private institution lending to the state in the 17th century. Over Europe loomed the House of Rothschild, and others subsequently. The Napoleonic war plunged Europe into colossal debt with its subsequent social, moral and political devastation. It set the pattern for the "modern age." An era of revolutionary upheaval throughout Europe, and reaching to the far off colonies, ending with Napoleon's defeat in 1815, saw the Rothschilds and other money-lenders as the real masters of Europe. While Metternich of Austria tried to establish a new social order for Europe based around Throne and Altar, the real rulers would henceforth be the bankers. Historian Adam Zamoyski writes:

> "Every government in Europe taxed whatever it could to pay off war-time borrowing. Britain had spent more in real terms than it would on the First World War, and its national debt was astronomical. Russia's had multiplied by twenty times between 1801 and 1809, and would more than double again by 1822. Austria was technically bankrupt: over the next three decades an average of 30 per cent of state revenue would be siphoned off to service this debt." (Zamoyski, *Phantom Terror*, Harper Collins, London 2014, 97).

Zamoyski states that the five Rothschild brothers, (who had been placed strategically throughout the capitals of Europe by their father, Mayer Amschel Rothschild), "and particularly James in Paris and

Salomon in Vienna, had lent most of the governments of Europe, and particularly those of Austria and France, large sums of money in return for government bonds... Metternich had close links with Rothschild, who had resolved many difficulties for him in the past and who had now arranged for his mother-in-law's 400,000-franc debt to be written off." (Ibid., 384-385). As for the traditional bulwark against usury, the Church, "The Papal states were bankrupt by 1832, and Metternich saved the pope by persuading the Viennese banking house of Rothschild to provide him with a loan." (Ibid., 473).

Awakening

The Great Depression spurred a widespread awakening among all sectors of society as to the character of the banking system. Proponents of a "new" (yet traditional) economics began appearing in many lands across the world at around the same time. During the 1930s Douglas' lectures on Social Credit impacted on nations from Britain, to Canada, from New Zealand to Japan and Norway and Australia. The famous New Zealand Labour politician John A. Lee remarked that the problems of credit and banking were discussed widely everywhere, in pubs, on buses, in the home. The First Labour Government in New Zealand was largely elected on the issue of banking. Who now, in this era of universal communications and education, gives five minutes to such questions, especially in pondering how to exercise one's futile vote? Our grandparents and great grandparents, although they might not have gone to school beyond the primary level, knew immensely more about such matters than subsequent generations. They saw the effects of "poverty amongst plenty," which showed a matter that has still not been resolved: that there are insufficient tokens ("money" and "credit") available to consume the entirety of production.

While many turned to communism and other forms of socialism, with their banal slogans, others turned to the "new economics" that alone hit at the root of the evil. Green Shirts marched in Britain behind drums and banners. The "Nazis" – before Hitler—were originally founded to fight "interest-slavery." The traditional Church social doctrine condemning usury provided a major impetus for such liberation movements, often combining Social Credit and similar theories. In Quebec since the 1930s, the Pilgrims of Saint Michael have combined Catholicism and Social Credit, and they remain among the few to continue the great crusading zeal of those times to the present. In the USA Father Charles Coughlin founded a great movement for the liberation of the USA from the bondage of interest-slavery, and millions listened to his message.

The Eternal Problem

Brooks Adams in his *Law of Civilisation and Decay* showed that the character of a civilisation can be discerned in its attitude towards credit and currency. Those societies that expend their innate store of collective energies on commerce are not known for splendid cultural achievements. In our own time, the USA might immediately come to mind. Once money-thinking became the dominant preoccupation of a society it becomes culturally enervated. Its *elan vital* or *libido*, in psychological terms, one might say, is channelled into money-oriented preoccupations and away from the founding traditions of the culture. The arts themselves become commodities; very evident in our era, like money has become a commodity. Oswald Spengler a few decades later in his *Decline of The West*, showed that money-thinking dominates in societies in their last era of development before collapse.

Adams can be read profitably with Spengler. For poet Ezra Pound, Brooks Adams had shown the importance of money and banking in distorting and corrupting the cultural life of society. John Hargrave who started a woodcraft movement, Kibbo Kift, as an alternative lifestyle for the young to the unhealthy and unnatural materialism and industrialisation of the modern era, came to Social Credit as the practical means by which society could be transformed.

Adams held that "commerce is antagonistic to the imagination." Where a state is commercially based, as are most states in the world today, aesthetics stagnates. Hence the great Gothic era that epitomises the flowering of Western Civilisation (what Spengler called the "Spring" epoch) did not flourish in the commercial city-states Venice, Genoa, Pisa, or Florence, "nor did any pure school of architecture thrive in the mercantile atmosphere." (Adams, *The Law of Civilization and Decay*, Macmillan, London, 1896, vi).

> "Whenever a race is so richly endowed with the energetic material that it does not expend all its energy in the daily struggle for life, the surplus may be stored in the shape of wealth; and this Stock of Stored energy may be transferred from community to community, either by conquest, or by superiority in economic competition. However large may be the store of energy accumulated by conquest,

a race must, sooner or later, reach the limit of its martial energy, when it must enter on the phase of economic competition. But, as the economic organism radically differs from the emotional and martial, the effect of economic competition has been, perhaps invariably, to dissipate the energy amassed by war."

"When surplus energy has accumulated in such bulk as to preponderate over productive energy, it becomes the controlling social force. Thenceforward, capital is autocratic, and energy vents itself through those organisms best fitted to give expression to the power of capital. In this last stage of consolidation, the economic, and, perhaps, the scientific intellect is propagated, while the imagination fades, and the emotional, the martial, and the artistic types of manhood decay."

"When a social velocity has been attained at which the waste of energetic material is so great that the martial and imaginative stocks fail to reproduce themselves, intensifying competition appears to generate two extreme economic types, — the usurer in his most formidable aspect, and the peasant whose nervous system is best adapted to thrive on scanty nutriment. At length a point must be reached when pressure can go no further, and then, perhaps, one of two results may follow: A stationary period may supervene, which may last until ended by war, by exhaustion, or by both combined, as seems to have been the case with the Eastern Empire; or, as in the Western, disintegration may set in, the civilized population may perish, and a reversion may take place to a primitive form of organism."

"The evidence, however, seems to point to the conclusion that, when a highly centralized society disintegrates, under the pressure of economic competition, it is because the energy of the race has been exhausted. Consequently, the survivors of such a community lack the power necessary for renewed concentration, and must probably remain inert until supplied with fresh energetic material by the infusion of barbarian blood." (Ibid., x).

Hence, as Ezra Pound realised from the aesthete's outlook there is more to the economic question than economics or politics alone. Pound knew exactly what processes were at work in eating away at the cultural organism. Pound's "With Usura" (*Canto XLV*) reflects lucidly the manner by which the primacy of money, as shown by Spengler and Adams, intervenes in the culture of a society, acting as a contagion on

Introduction

the social organism, on work, craft, art, religion, and all else associated with a High Culture:

> With usura no picture is made to endure
> nor to live with but it is made to sell and to sell quickly...
> Stone cutter is kept from his stone
> Weaver is kept from his loom...
> WITH USURA
> Wool comes not to market
> Sheep bring not gain with usura...
> Usura rusteth the chisel
> It rusteth the craft and the craftsman...

The issue is the most vital of all as Feder contended. It strikes at the root of all problems. The "Right" has forgotten this. The "Left' could never realise it. Today we see how readily the Leftist Syriza Party succumbed to the international bankers when assuming Office in Greece. This is the historic replay of orthodox Leftism in the service of Mammon. The Bible references "Mammon" as "a root of all kinds of evils":

> "But those who desire to be rich fall into temptation, into a snare, into many senseless and harmful desires that plunge people into ruin and destruction. For the love of money is a root of all kinds of evils." (I Tim. 6:9-10).

This is the key of history. It is the root cause beyond both biological determinism and dialectical materialism. For our era and our Civilisation there remains one figure, one archetype, one symbol, that of Christ pursuing the money-changers from the Temple, scourge in hand, scattering their tables, their counters, their coins. (Matt. 21:12). That this subject once commanded the primary attention of millions of folk of all stations of life, around the world, and led to the fall and rise of governments, is now difficult to imagine, at a time when education and information are as universal as the accompanying ignorance and lethargy of the modern era.

"The trade of the petty usurer is hated with most reason: it makes a profit from currency itself, instead of making it from the process which currency was meant to serve."— Aristotle (384-322 BC)

Arthur Nelson Field

Arthur Nelson Field

Arthur Nelson Field will be a name more familiar to monetary reformers in the USA, Britain and Australia than in his native New Zealand. I would be surprised if there were more than a dozen people in New Zealand who are familiar with his life and works. Yet he was the scion of a pioneering family well known in commerce and politics, and made an early name for himself as a journalist. During the Depression era, he became a leading authority and best-selling author on banking and monetary reform and was widely recognised as such.

Field lived during an era when being proud of the "British race" was the norm, the Jewish issue could be discussed and sympathy for "fascism' did not automatically put one beyond the pale of polite society; indeed it was widely admitted in polite society. Most importantly banking reform was a crucial political issue in New Zealand, especially after Major C. H. Douglas toured, propounding his Social Credit theory. Ironically, Field did not follow Social Credit, but advocated the prior banking reform theories of Arthur Kitson, a British inventor and businessmen, whose answer to financial and economic crises was what most closely resembles today the ridiculed 'fiat money' or 'quantitative easing', which we are assured causes disastrous inflation Zimbabwe-style.

A biographical note that was intended for circulation with his 1957 book *The Bretton Woods Plot* states that Field was born in Nelson in 1882 and went into journalism in 1900. He was a sub-editor for Wellington's *Evening Post*, *The Dominion* and other newspapers in New Zealand and Australia. Apart from the mainstream press, Field also published his own periodicals, the first being *The Citizen*, started in 1909, followed by *God's Own Country* in 1932, and then *The Examiner*.

Enlisting in 1915 he served as Lance Corporal with the New Zealand Expeditionary Force in Flanders in 1916 where he was wounded in the hip by shrapnel and discharged. The exploits of a scion of this famous family were closely followed by the press. Despite his injuries, he returned to active service with the Navy, as a Sub-Lieutenant on the HMS Spencer.

Arthur Nelson Field

Truth About The Slump

Leaving *The Dominion* in 1928 to assume management of a heavily indebted farm owned by his father and uncle, Field was brought up-close to the debt finance system. He began writing articles on "the monetary question" in 1930, a year during which there were about 30,000 unemployed in New Zealand. He was particularly interested in the monetary proposals of Professor Irving Fisher in the USA, Dr. Gustav Cassel in Sweden, and Arthur Kitson. (Field, *"The Bretton Woods Plot, How it Came to be Written"*).

The first series of articles he wrote on finance were entitled "Wobbling Money," published by *The Dominion*. This coincided with the year that Bank of England director Sir Otto Niemeyer and Professor Theodore Gregory of the London School of Economics, came to New Zealand and Australia to advise on economic matters, and the setting up of a central bank controlled by private bond-holders. The visits were widely regarded in both countries as intrusions by the "Money Power" and drew condemnation from elements of both Left and Right, bringing New South Wales close to civil war when Labor Premier Jack Lang resisted. The Niemeyer-Gregory visit prompted Field to undertake extensive research.

Despite the popularity of Major C. H. Douglas' Social Credit theory in New Zealand, Field looked to Arthur Kitson, who had published his first book, *The Money Question*, in 1893, preceding Douglas' Social Credit by several decades. Kitson wrote:

> "Under the system I propose, variations in supply and demand of money could have no effect upon prices, because the supply would be always ample to meet the demand. By making all commodities equal — that is, putting them on the same footing — all would be alike monetizable. Industry, trade and commerce would then assume their natural position and become independent of finance. The fortunes of manufacturers and merchants would then cease to be the shuttlecocks of money brokers and speculators."

Field had a collection of Kitson's books, but only one by Douglas (*Credit Power & Democracy*, 1921). Among the former were *The Money Question* (1903), *Money Problems* (1920), *Unemployment: the Cause & Remedy* (1921), *The Bankers' Conspiracy* (1933), and *A Modern Pilgrim's Progress by a Fellow Pilgrim* (1935).

Opposing the Money Lenders

Field's first book was *The Truth About The Slump*, published in 1931. The book was a best-seller in New Zealand and Australia. It was sought after among the burgeoning Australian Social Credit circles. Hon. Les H. Hollins, a Social Credit stalwart serving in the Victorian State Legislative Assembly 1940-1945, and as a State Minister in the short-lived McFarlane Government in 1945, drew heavily from *The Truth About The Slump* for his book *Democracy at the Crossroads*. (1934) He returned to *The Truth About The Slump* in 1949 for his *Only One Road*. (1949).

Field was also a seminal influence on the Australian League of Rights, despite the League's commitment to Douglas Social Credit. A community newspaper was to emerge as the long-running magazine *New Times* published by the League. Tasmanian Labor Senator Richard Darcey wrote to Field in 1939 praising *The Truth About The Slump*. In 1931 Harry Atmore, Member of Parliament for Nelson, recommended the book in the House as exposing "the international financial jugglers." During the same session of the House, Labour's Bob Semple, who became Minister of Works and of National Service during World War II, praised Field's "great book" which exposes "that group of individuals which control the international finances of the world." It seems odd today that back then stalwarts of both the Left and the Right could unite on the need to overcome the shylocks.

In the introduction to *The Truth About the Slump*, Field acknowledged Kitson, quoting from a 1925 article appearing in England's *National Review*, that "the mysteries of money" will never be understood unless it is realised that "money lending is a business run solely for the profit of the moneylenders." Much of the book is concerned with exposing the identity of the bankers manipulating the world financial system; in particular Paul Warburg of Kuhn, Loeb & Co. architect of the Federal Reserve Bank in the USA.

In 1936 in *All These Things* Field begins with what was the defining event in the political thinking of many New Zealanders and Australians, the arrival of the Bank of England's "emissaries," Niemeyer and Gregory. This history of the role of the banking interests throughout the world provided the basis for Field's recommendation for banking reform to both free New Zealand from the thrall of international finance and to establish a system that would provide security and prosperity. Like John A. Lee, Field pointed out that the Labour Party had been elected to Government mainly on their promises of banking reform, and that the Reserve Bank Act of 1936 provided a good start in placing the Bank under the authority of Parliament. Yet, the new Labour Government did not adequately define the role of the Bank. What was required, and what was never enacted, was: "1. The institution of Government money maintained in sufficient supply for the needs of the people, and so regulated as to have a constant debt-paying, purchasing power; and (2) the extinction of the public debt of the country."

In 1939 Field wrote a book specifically on the machinations of bankers in New Zealand history, *The Truth About New Zealand*. It is a book that could teach New Zealanders a lot about the hidden past that explains the present. Field traces the origins of the New Zealand Colony to the manoeuvres of the New Zealand Company, a private entity that was set up to open New Zealand for settlement, drawing on the desperation of the poor of Britain who hoped to find a paradise here, as per the depictions by New Zealand Company publicity. When the New Zealand Company relinquished its charter to the Crown in 1850 it had sold millions of acres of land it did not own [as did wily Maori chiefs who sold land they did not own to the New Zealand Company and those who came after]. In 1856 the colonists of the first assembly "were obliged to raise a loan in London to extinguish the company's claim on the colony for £200,000, which claim the Crown commissioner on the company's board had described as established 'by gross frauds,' concealments, and misrepresentations..." Others reached New Zealand, able to buy large blocks of land at low prices, and sell them at prices sufficiently to entice the poorer elements, who had to borrow from moneylenders at 10% to 20%.

The founding of the Bank of New Zealand (BNZ) in 1860 was a defining moment. It is what Field described by the title of chapter two as "The Power Behind the Throne." The BNZ quickly got the Government account. Frederick Whitaker, solicitor of the bank during 1861-1889, was also over that period twice Premier, five times Attorney-General, and once Postmaster-General. His partner in the BNZ, Thomas Russell, was in Parliament during 1861-1867, and during part of the Maori Land War held the post of Minister of Colonial Defence.

What Field next described is crucial to understanding New Zealand history and especially New Zealand race relations to the present. On advice from Whitaker as Attorney-General, who stated that the land in Taranaki that was under dispute, had been legally bought by the Crown, a land war resulted that extended from Taranaki Province to Auckland. Subsequent advice obtained by Sir George Grey, who had been hurriedly sent back to New Zealand as Governor, was that

Opposing the Money Lenders

Whitaker's counsel had been unsound. The discovery was too late, and 10,000 troops mobilised for a campaign that lasted ten years. This cost the young colony up to £4,000,000. New Zealand's second loan was floated to pay for the war via the BNZ, but the expenditure of much of it was never recorded. One of the items of expenditure was the supply of hay to the Imperial troops. The contractor was Thomas Russell's brother-in-law. The Weld Ministry cancelled the contract, regarding the price as excessive, but the contractor had bought up all the hay in the market and the Government was obliged to pay him double the original price. Following this transaction, Russell went into partnership with his bother-in-law in a 30,000 acre property in the South Island.

The banking sector thrived during the Land Wars, while the tumult was kept going by business interests selling arms to the Maori. What happened to confiscated Maori land after the war is a story of gross exploitation, but not for the general benefit of the colonists. The land was supposed to be offered at public auction at a minimum of 5 shillings per acre. However, under the administration of Julius Vogel, Russell and some of his banking colleagues purchased the Piako block of over 80,000 acres privately for 2s. 6d. per acre. The Patatere block of 250,000 acres was acquired on similar terms by Whitaker and Russell. Another block of 150,000 acres east of Piako was floated by Russell into the Thames Valley Land Company.

When ex-Governor Grey entered Parliament to oppose the policies of Vogel, Grey declared in 1883: "One great central power in New Zealand oppresses it from end to end. That central power is moved by the Premier, and the Premier is the solicitor of these great moneyed corporations. Is it just? Does it give the people of New Zealand a fair chance? As long as this continues I see no hope for ourselves or our country." (Field, ibid.).

Vogel became Premier in 1873 and, without informing Parliament, in 1874 went to England with Russell, and floated a loan of £4,000,000 at 4.5% with Messrs Rothschild. He then spent 16 months in Europe "at the Continental casinos of Homburg and Wiesbaden," for which he tried to claim £8390 expenses, although Parliament, to his indignation, slashed off £2750. "By 1876 Vogelism had resulted in the annual charges on the public debt swallowing up about two-thirds of the revenue, and bankruptcy was imminent." (Field, ibid.).

Arthur Nelson Field

The Examiner

Field founded the *Examiner* in 1937, named after the first settler newspaper in Nelson. The *Examiner* was a mixture of news and in depth features, some of which became the basis of books such as *Socialism Without The Mask* (1938).

The need for monetary reform remained the focus of the *Examiner*. What was happening around the world had much to do with the machinations of international finance. A four page supplement, "Money is Smashing Civilization," gave an historical outline of money from the time of 600BC Greece. Tracing coinage in England from King Offa of Mercia, 775AD, through the Medieval era, Field noted that booms and busts had been absent for centuries, not because of the superiority of metal coinage over paper money, but because the Crown maintained a "sufficient quantity of money in circulation for the people's needs." Prices maintained their stability for several hundred years. The introduction of banking practises after 1650 destroyed this stability.

> "History shows that during the six and a half centuries from the Norman Conquest until the bankers and speculators came in the middle of the seventeenth century, the kings of England gave the people of England money that was stable in its purchasing power and in plenty for their needs." ('Honest King's Money', *Examiner*, No. 6).

The problem with the financial system was that of usury. The solution was ultimately a Christian one, because the basis of Christian institutions is the "principle of Duty." The "whole framework embodied the idea that ownership of property is a social function to be exercised for the common good. The ideal behind feudalism was stewardship, with a sequence of duty from the highest to the lowest." The Chivalry of a Knight, if not always adhered to, was nonetheless a noble idea demanding commitment to 26 oaths emphasising humility, charity, and service to the weak.

The standard of living of Medieval England had been better than that of the worker hundreds of years later, as noted by the 19th Century social commentator William Cobbett. This long regime of relative justice and prosperity came to an end with the Reformation which, under the guise of opposing alleged Church abuses, was motivated by self-interest; confiscated Church lands being parcelled out to

Henry's sycophants. For the first time beggars filled the land. Usury was legalised by Henry VIII in 1545. In 1600 land became a freely marketable commodity, and any ethic of social responsibility of ownership became redundant.

Field believed that the basis of the nation was the land. He had begun to study financial matters after being embroiled with the indebted farm of his father and uncle. National Socialist Germany's policies for farms were of particular interest. Neither National nor Labour Governments had done anything to secure New Zealand farmers from the usurer and the speculator. Germany's Hereditary Freehold Farms Law of 1933 ensured that a farm could not be foreclosed, that farms were inherited within the family, and that if a farmer proved inefficient his farm would nonetheless be handed over to his wife or other kin. Field concluded: "When a patriotic New Zealand Government comes to lift the farmers of this Dominion out of the slough of debt and put them at long last in genuine possession of their farms, some parts of this German law may be worth studying." ("Farms with no Mortgage: Interesting German Law," *Examiner*, No. 6).

The Crusade

In 1932 Harry Atmore, M.P. for Nelson, urged the Prime Minister, attending the Otawa Conference, to be accompanied by Field as his financial adviser. Atmore stated that someone was required who supported the unorthodox financial proposals of Cassel, Soddy, et al. ("Mr Atmore's suggestion," *Evening Post*, 1 June 1932). It is a measure of the extent to which Field was acknowledged as an authority on banking. In 1931, *The Evening Post* reported:

> "A resolution urging that the Government should make an investigation of the money stabilisation plan of Professor Irving Fisher, as recommended by the New Zealand Board of Trade in its annual report in 1919, was adopted by the Nelson provincial executive of the Farmers' Union following an address by Mr A N Field.... The executive decided unanimously to support the request for an examination of Professor Fisher's plan, also to request the National Economic Committee, about to sit in Wellington, to hear Mr Field." ("Stabilising Money," *Evening Post*, 18 February 1931).

The Farmers' Union resolution is indicative of the widespread demand for monetary reform that led to a Labour victory. The Auckland

Arthur Nelson Field

Farmers' Union adopted a Social Credit policy around this time, a policy that was zealously proselytised by the poet Rex Fairburn who assumed editorship of its newspaper *Farming First*.

In 1932 Field and Atmore teamed up to promote monetary reform. The *Evening Post* report is worth quoting extensively as it succinctly explains Field's ideas:

"MR. FIELD'S SOLUTION USING OUR OWN CREDIT

The establishment of a Currency Control Board, with the sole right to issue notes, was the main suggestion made by Mr. A. N. Field. When in company with Mr H Atmore, M.P. for Nelson, he addressed a meeting of nearly two thousand people in the Town Hall last evening. Mr. Atmore spoke much on the lines of previous addresses, urging the necessity for New Zealand to use its own credit.

"The meeting was held under the auspices of the New Economies Research Association. The following motion was carried:—

"That this mass meeting of Wellington citizens, after hearing the statements of Messrs. H. Atmore, M.P., and A. N. Field, is convinced that immediate action should be taken by the Government to the following ends:—

1. The establishment of a Currency Control Board with sole right of note issue, and with absolute control of credit.

2. The issue of sufficient money by the Currency Control Board to restore normal conditions in agriculture, industry, and employment by liberalising the distribution of money, thus liberalising the distribution of production.

3. The regulation thereafter by the Currency Control Board of the quantity of money in circulation so as to maintain a stable price level within the Dominion.

4. That it is the function of the State to maintain conditions under which all citizens have the opportunity of engaging in remunerative labour, and that all should have security from the fear of want in age and disability.

Opposing the Money Lenders

"MASTER IN ITS OWN HOUSE.

Mr. Field said that the only answer for our troubles was for the State to be master in its own house. That the State could never be so long as the control of money, the measure of value, was farmed out to private interests. There was no shortage of real wealth in the world. They lived in an age of plenty. What lunacy, then, was it that prevented them from enjoying that plenty? ...

"The way to get rid of the slump was for the State to take control of the money system and issue sufficient money to restore normal conditions in agriculture, industry, and employment, and thereafter so to regulate money as to keep values on a steady level. New Zealand had nothing to lose and everything to gain by regulating their money market to suit themselves. Money had no value in itself. 'It was merely a ticket entitling the bearer to goods and services. If the quantity of money in circulation were increased prices would tend to go up. That meant that people would be able to pay their debts, that employers could pay decent wages, and that trade would revive and unemployment decrease."

("Currency Board way out of Slump. Mr Field's Solution. Using our own Credit," *Evening Post*, 19 August 1932).

Several months after the Wellington meeting with Atmore, Field and Captain Rushworth, Member of Parliament for the Country Party, convened a conference of thirty-three associations of the Currency and Monetary Reform Leagues. This was chaired by General Sir Andrew Russell, president of the Returned Soldiers' Association, who became Inspector-General of the New Zealand Military Force during World War II, and now one of New Zealand's most celebrated military men. (It is notable that a recent biography of Russell has scant mention of his role in advocating monetary reform).

Rushworth "formally moved the first principle of the right of self-government in finance through Parliament, stating that there was no middle course between control by the people through Parliament and Bank of England control." The conference resolved to form the Federation of Monetary Reform Associations under the presidency of Sir Andrew. ("Monetary Reform Federation set up.

Request for an Inquiry," *Evening Post*, 21 October 1932).

Arthur Nelson Field

The New Zealand Legion

In 1932 Field thought more vigorous action was required to save New Zealand, and had talks with disaffected members of the governing Reform Party, in the wake of riots by unemployed. The United-Reform coalition government was incapable of dealing with the situation. These dissident elements formed the New Zealand National Movement led by Field's friend Major J. R. V. Sherston. This was renamed the New Zealand Legion, reaching 20,000 members under the leadership of the popular Wellington surgeon Dr. Campbell Begg. Field's own group, the National Security League, was incorporated into the Legion. General Sir Andrew Russell was also a Legionnaire. In November 1933, the Economic Research Division of the Legion's Wellington District recommended that the State should control money, credit and land. But it caused opposition from factions within, which saw anything of the kind as socialism.

Field's ideas were the major source for the Legion's economic programme. Although Begg met C. H. Douglas twice during the latter's New Zealand tour, that was in 1934, and the initial economic program had been released in 1933. That year the Legion's journal *National Opinion* carried a front page article on the Niemeyer and Gregory proposals for a Reserve Bank, pointing out that this would become an appendage of the Bank of England. The central banks of England, USA, Germany and France controlled the currency and credit of the world. Many of the directors of the Bank of England 'have a greater claim to be regarded as international financiers than British, and one may doubt whether some of them have any more real loyalty to the British Empire than to any other country'. The article quotes Professor Soddy that "there cannot be any compromise, it must be either the government or the banks," and continued: "Currency and credit are the vehicle of production, distribution and exchange, and whoever controls those controls the very basis of the nation's existence." The sovereign rights of the people are being made "playthings of the international financiers." (C.R.C. Robieson, "Niemeyer – Empire Dictator," *National Opinion*, 7 September 1933). In 1934 *National Opinion* carried a picture of C. H. Douglas on its front page, and the Legion's programme, including "control of currency by the State." ('The Legion's 12 Points', *National Opinion*, 1 March 1934). With opposition from regressive forces of Left and Right and factionalism within its own ranks, the Legion sank to oblivion within several years, but the interest in banking reform did not.

Opposing the Money Lenders

Throughout the 1930s Field was a widely reported speaker before Parliamentary hearings on finance. One newspaper report states:

> "... For example, let us take the views of A. N. Field, easily the ablest monetary reform writer in New Zealand. In a fairly comprehensive pamphlet written for the National Security League Mr Field did not by any means rush straightway into monetary reform; he is too well-informed for that. After an introductory paragraph, the burden of which is that the aim of the State should be the welfare of its individual constituent members, Mr Field deals trenchantly with the land question, gives this pride of place, and then takes the monetary issue in its proper order, second: 'Land and money, therefore, are the two urgent problems with which we have to deal.' ..." ("Politics and Economics," *Ellesmere Guardian*, 14 January 1936).

World War & Security Intelligence Response

With the outbreak of war there were some questions raised as to Field's loyalties. He had often cited Germany's "World Service" news network in the *Examiner*, for example. In Australia, Field's contacts prompted belated interest from the Commonwealth Security Service in Canberra.

On 24 December 1943 the New Zealand Security Intelligence Bureau sent a confidential memorandum to the New Zealand Legation in Washington commenting that Field "is extremely well-known in New Zealand as an ardent authority on banking and finance." The memorandum was in response to an enquiry about Field from British Security Co-ordination in Washington. The memorandum refers to *The Truth About the Slump* having "had considerable vogue and influence in this country some ten years ago." However, A. D. McIntosh, Secretary to the War Cabinet and author of the memorandum, commented that "Security authorities in New Zealand have seen no reason to take any particular action against him, though they have investigated his activities very exhaustively."

On 15 December a five-page report on Field was compiled by Security Intelligence for McIntosh. This report referred to Field's 'distinguished career' in journalism. His books even then were considered to have enjoyed as much attention outside New Zealand as within and perhaps more so. 'He is undoubtedly a widely-read man, with a great

Arthur Nelson Field

capacity for research, and has devoted much of his life to a study of finance, in particular." *The Truth About New Zealand* is described as "a highly-documented publication [and] is in itself proof enough of a quite extraordinary capacity for research." Field was "prophetic' in his pre-World War I journal *The Citizen* on the Empire's lack of preparedness for a coming war against Germany, and of the growing naval menace of Japan. A concern was with Field's association with the Australian Unity League, regarded as anti-Semitic and pro-fascist, which had published *The Truth About the Slump*, and his citing of other fascist sources from around the world. He was however noted as having a particular loyalty to the Crown, and was not regarded as a security threat. ("Arthur Nelson Field," 15 December 1943). Field was spared the fate of hundreds in Britain, many of whom had also been World War I veterans but were subsequently detained by the British Government without charge or trial during World War Two.

The Post-War Legacy

When Field died on 3 January 1963 the only acknowledgement was a few lines in the obituary column of the *Nelson Evening Mail*. But Field has had a lasting legacy on monetary reform, although forgotten by all but a few in New Zealand. Many of his books have remained in publication, since Omni Publications (USA) started issuing editions in the 1960s. Of particular significance was the influence of Field on the thinking of two eminent campaigners for the British and broader Western heritage in opposition to international finance. Eric Butler, the pre-eminent campaigner for Social Credit in Australia for decades, wrote of Field after reading *The Truth About New Zealand*, which he reviewed in the *New Times* in 1939:

> "Those who have studied the writings of A N Field, the well known New Zealand writer in finance and the part it plays in national and international affairs, will welcome his latest book, as a carefully compiled, and detailed answer to the many questions which arise concerning the Labour Party administration of our sister dominion."

Another important personality influenced by Field was A. K. Chesterton, a Fleet Street journalist, who had briefly served in Mosley's British Union of Fascists. In 1953 Chesterton established the magazine *Candour*, which continues to the present day, and the League of Empire Loyalists, noted during the 1950s and 1960s for its audacious protests against the sell-out of British interests. Writing in *Candour* after Chesterton's death, Kevan Bleach recalled :

> "*Candour's* founder, and editor for twenty years, A K Chesterton, wrote several times reminiscing how, in the period before the First World War he heard Labour Party speakers constantly harangue about the evils of international finance. Then strangely, in the years following that war, the finance-capitalists were attacked no more – the wrath of socialist speakers being directed solely at *industrial* capitalists, the captains of industry. It was not until his conversations with authorities like A N Field and Arthur Kitson in the early 'thirties that he came to realise, beyond all possibility of informed contradiction, the direct link between international finance and an international socialism. ("Conspirators All," *Candour* article reprint, n.d., Candour Publishing Co. Forest House, Liss Forest, Hants).

Hence, Field had been a seminal influence on the early political education of A. K. Chesterton, himself one of the finest writers on the subversion of the British Empire and of Western Civilisation by international finance. When in 1965 Chesterton wrote his primer, *The New Unhappy Lords* on the subversion of the European empires by the largely U.S.-based "Money Power," he included in the bibliography *The Truth About The Slump*. He commented: "Those books in this section will prove useful to the reader who wishes to extend his study of the theme advanced in *The New Unhappy Lords*. Those by the late A N Field are recommended without mental reservation."

Posthumously, Field's works have been kept in print. *All These Things* was republished by Omni in 1963. The Australian League of Rights, which continues the legacy of Field's friend Eric Butler, has published Field's titles through Veritas Books, and carries Field's *Bretton Woods Plot*, *Truth About New Zealand*, and *Untaught History of Money*.

The following three essays appeared in Field's journal *God's Own Country (And the Devil's Own Mess)*. Two of the articles show the efficacy of the now derided 'fiat money', one on contemporary Sweden, another on 17th Century French Canada.

Arthur Nelson Field

The Next Best Thing

Paper Money Better than No Money

TWO and a half centuries ago the people of French Canada found themselves up against much the same sort of situation that faces us in New Zealand today. We depend on receiving a large supply of money from London each year from the sale of our produce there. In French Canada they depended on receiving a substantial remittance from the Government in Paris each year. In the year 1685, King Louis XIV being busy with his wars, his craze for building palaces, his mistresses, and the rest of his extravagances, the Canadian remittance failed to arrive.

Had the Intendant of French Canada been versed in modern economic principles, he would have proceeded to meet the situation by that interesting process known as "balancing the budget." That is to say, the people of Canada having much less money than usual, he would have taken from them much more than usual in taxes. He would have disbanded his troops, discharged as many public servants as possible, and the business people would likewise have been forced to dismiss their workmen, not having the wherewithal to pay them. This horde of workless persons, deprived of the means of subsistence, would have to be kept alive somehow, and no doubt still further taxes would have been imposed to provide a pittance to enable them to keep body and soul together. That is what is called "balancing the budget" Another name for it is Making Bad go to Worse.

It was a lucky thing for French Canada that its Intendant knew nothing of economics. Being a plain, sensible man, his first action was to draw on all the money at his disposal. This proving totally insufficient, he used the first substitute he could think of, and got about his business without more ado. In other words, he acted on ordinary, commonsense principles. A certain commodity, money, not being to hand he made shift with the next best thing. He manufactured some temporary, makeshift, substitute money. He had not even a printing press to do it with. That did not stop him. He called in all the packs of playing cards he could get hold of, took a pair of scissors and cut them into quarters, wrote on these scraps of pasteboard the amount of money each was supposed to represent, and paid the Government expenses with them. Here is the story of the Intendant, M. de Meulle, in his own words as written on September 24th, 1685, in his report to the Minister in Paris:—

Opposing the Money Lenders

"I have drawn from my own funds and from those of my friends, all I have been able to get, but at last finding them without means of rendering me further assistance, and not knowing to what saint to pay my vows, money being extremely scarce, having distributed considerable sums on every side for the pay of the soldiers, it occurred to me to issue, instead of money, notes on cards, which I have had cut into quarters. I send you, my Lord, the three kinds. ... I have issued an ordinance by which I have obliged all the inhabitants to receive this money in payment, and to give it circulation, at the same time pledging myself in my own name to redeem the said notes. No person has refused them, and so good has been the effect that by this means the troops have lived as usual."

Will you please note and remember that last statement... "the troops have lived as usual." Six years later, there was again a shortage of money in Canada, and for a second time resort was made to playing card money. "It became exceedingly popular," writes Mr. Norman Angell in *"The Story of Money"* published last year, "and remained current during the whole of the remainder of that century, and the first half of the next." As late as 1749 ordinances were passed in Canada increasing the issue to a million livres. The French Government made repeated protests against the issue of this money, but the Canadians found it served its purpose, and much preferred using makeshift money to plunging into bankruptcy with no money at all. Their exchange depreciated to some extent (ours has done that already). As one historian says:

"It was true that the people of Canada had to pay more in this currency than in coined money for their supplies from France, but when the whole kingdom was in distress it was only fair that the Canadians should share in the sufferings and disadvantages."

This is not a fairy tale. It is actual recorded, historical fact, the full details of which are preserved in the archives of Canada. The French Canadians did not live quite as well with their playing-card money as with coined money, for they paid more for goods brought from France. But they lived very much better than they could ever have hoped to live without it. The makeshift worked, and the people went about their business as usual. What M. de Meulle did was a very simple thing. At the same time it was a very profound thing. M. de Meulle probably never considered that there was anything very profound about it. It was just an obvious, commonsense step; and it was the right step.

Arthur Nelson Field

Money is merely a ticket entitling the bearer to goods and services, and it matters little whether it is made of gold or cut up out of playing cards. Even a filthy bit of crumpled, smelly paper will serve, as we know in New Zealand. The essential thing is that it should be backed by the credit of the State—it is quite sufficient that the State accepts it in payment of taxes—and that the quantity of it issued is so regulated that the general level of prices keeps on an even keel.

The steps that were taken by M. de Meulle in Canada in 1685 could be taken by the Parliament of New Zealand tomorrow if it wished, and there is not the least reason to fear any less satisfactory results.

Parliament does not take any such step because it is the slave of false ideas, false ideas that are strangling and choking our civilisation. Because of these ideas we remain in a stupid slump that we could walk out of if we chose.

Lending Money that Does Not Exist

THE world's troubles today arise from the fact that its bankers have been permitted to build up their businesses on the basis of lending money they do not possess.

How this came about is a long story, but its outlines can be given briefly. Up to the seventeenth century the merchants of London used to store their gold for safe-keeping in the Tower of London, but Charles I, on the advice of Lord Cottington, seized £200,000 of this gold as a loan. It was paid back, but the same thing occurred again, and faith in the Tower of London as a safe deposit waned.

In what is now known as Lombard Street there were at this time a number of Jewish goldsmiths from Lombardy, between thirty and forty of them. They had strong vaults and a good reputation for honesty, and they got the job of storing the merchants' gold. To settle their accounts the merchants wrote out orders on the goldsmiths to pay out so much gold. Thus the cheque system began. The goldsmiths in many cases being better known than the merchants, it was also found a convenience to get receipts from them for gold deposited, such receipts being divided into convenient amounts and used for the payment of accounts. That was the origin of the modern bank-note.

Very soon the goldsmiths found they were doing quite a lot of business without actually passing out any great quantity of gold. Settlements were being made all the time by book entries, debiting one customer with so much gold paid out and crediting the amount to the customer receiving the payment.

The Goldsmiths Lead the Way.

The next thing that occurred was that when borrowers came applying for loans, the goldsmiths, instead of lending them actual gold gave them paper receipts or promises to pay them actual gold on demand. Presently the goldsmiths found it was pretty safe to issue paper for amounts in excess of the gold they actually possessed. They took the chance that no great number of their customers would come wanting the gold at once. As a writer in 1695 put it: "No goldsmith hath in his vaults guineas and crowns to the full value of his paper."

It is on this basis of lending money that has no material existence whatsoever that our modern banking business has been built up. That process has proceeded to prodigious lengths.

The early banks in Britain came to grief so frequently that stringent laws were made about the gold backing for their note issue in order to protect the public. But it never seemed to strike anybody that it was just as necessary to see that the cheque money was also protected. The cheque-writing habit grew gradually. Today cheque money is the most important of all and is used for the great bulk of payments made. Behind it there is nothing tangible at all, and the greater part of our stock of money today is nothing but figures in bank books.

Take the case of the £116 millions of money in New Zealand. Of this £6 millions is bank notes in circulation, £57 millions is money on deposit in the trading banks, and £53 millions is in the savings banks. In addition there is also an unknown quantity of silver and copper coins in circulation.

What tangible existence has this £116 millions of money? If you examine the published returns you will find that the banks hold against it about £7 millions of "coin and bullion' The other £109 millions is nothing but paper and figures in bank books.

Arthur Nelson Field

The Emperor's New Clothes.

Most people think of bank deposits coming into existence in consequence of people taking actual hard cash and paying it into the banks. In reality only a very small proportion of the total originates in this way. The rest is manufactured by the banks out of the same material as the emperor's new clothes in Hans Andersen's fairy tales.

In that "very human little" story we are told how two strangers arrived in the capital city and gave out that they were weavers who could weave the most beautiful cloth ever made. This cloth, they said, had the singular property that no one unfit for his office could see it.

The emperor thought it a good idea to possess such wonderful clothing, so he sent his old Chancellor to inspect it. The Chancellor went but could see nothing in the looms. The old gentleman was terrified to go back and say he could see no cloth so he gave a glowing account of it.

The emperor then went to look at it and the swindlers took rolls of nothing down from empty shelves and unrolled them for the royal inspection. "Is it not magnificent?" said the old Chancellor.

The emperor could see nothing, but wouldn't admit it, and nodded in a condescending manner. As soon as he had done so all the courtiers in his suite exclaimed in a chorus, "Charming, elegant, exquisite!"

So the emperor ordered state robes to be made of the cloth for him to wear in a great procession about to take place. The swindlers then worked the looms harder than ever, and kept them going through the night with the building lit up, so that all the townspeople could see how hard they were working to finish the wonderful clothes for the emperor, which were now the talk of the town.

The next morning the emperor took off all his clothes and the swindlers pretended to clothe him in the new garments. "How beautifully they sit!" exclaimed the courtiers. "What an exquisite costume!"

And so the procession began with two chamberlains walking behind the emperor, just as if they were holding a train up in the air, for they dare not admit they could see nothing.

The emperor walked through the crowded streets and all the townspeople kept remarking to each other how beautiful his clothes were, for no one would allow for a minute that he could see nothing at all, for there was no knowing what his neighbours might think of him if he admitted that.

"But he has nothing on!" cried a little child at last. Its father tried to keep it quiet, but one after another the people began to whisper to each other the same truth, until at last they all shouted, "But he has nothing on!" That struck the emperor, for it appeared to him that they were right, but he thought to himself, "But I must go through with it now." And so the procession went on, and the chamberlains walked more stiffly than ever holding up the train that was not there.

It is a little odd to go to a book of fairy tales for a description of our modern monetary system. Perhaps the reader may think the position has been exaggerated. But such is not the case.

How Bank Deposits Originate.

In one of his addresses as chairman of the great Midland Bank in London the Rt. Hon. Reginald McKenna gave a very full account of how the banks make money out of nothing. His speech is reprinted in his little book "Post-War Banking." Professor Soddy, in his book "Money versus Man," also goes into it very fully.

A clear statement of the facts is also given in the report of the Committee on Finance and Industry set up by the British Government in 1929, and which finished its labours last year. This body, known as the Macmillan Committee, makes no bones about the fact that when the banks in Britain get hold of one pound in hard cash, they proceed to lend out £10 of which sum £9 has no tangible existence. Here is what these men, mostly bankers, say on page 34 of their report:—

> "It is not unnatural to think of the deposits of a bank as being created by the public through the deposit of cash representing either savings or amounts which are not for the time being required to meet expenditure. "But the bulk of the deposits arise out of the action of the banks themselves, for by granting loans, allowing money to be drawn on overdraft or purchasing securities a bank creates a credit in its books, which is the equivalent of a deposit.
>
> "A simple illustration, in which it will be convenient to assume

that all banking is concentrated in one bank, will make this clear.

"Let us suppose that a customer has paid into the bank £1,000 in cash and that it is judged from experience that only the equivalent of 10 per cent, of the bank deposit need be held actually in cash to meet the demands of customers; then the £1,000 cash will obviously support deposits amounting to £10,000.

"Suppose that the bank then grants a loan of £900; it will open a credit of £900 for its customer, and when the customer draws a cheque for £900 upon the credit so opened that cheque will, on our hypothesis, be paid into the account of another of the bank's customers.

"The bank now holds both the original deposit of £1,000 and the £900 paid in by the second customer. Deposits have thus increased to £1,900 and the bank holds against its liability to pay out this sum (a) the original £1,000 of cash deposited and (b) the obligation of a customer to repay-the loan of £900.

"The bank can carry on the process of lending .... until such time as the credits created represent nine times the amount of the original deposit of £1,000 in cash."

When the operations thus described are completed the bank will have lent £10,000 and of this sum £9,000 will be new money that had no previous existence. This money will have been created by the bank. Similarly, when the bank calls upon those to whom it has loaned this £9,000 to repay it, it will upon the cancellation of the loans be destroying money. As Mr. Reginald McKenna put it in his address already referred to:

"I am afraid the ordinary citizen will not like to be told that the banks (can and do) create and destroy money. The amount of money in existence varies only with the action of the banks in increasing or decreasing deposits. Every loan or overdraft creates a deposit, and every repayment of a loan or overdraft destroys a deposit." And he added later: "And they who control the credit of a nation, direct the policy of Governments, and hold in the hollow of their hands the destiny of the people."

Opposing the Money Lenders

Just the Same as Counterfeiting.

Here is the opinion of Professor Soddy, of Oxford University, as to what this means. The extract is from page 19 of his *"Money versus Man"*:—

> "The century that has come and gone has witnessed a practically complete reversal in the nature of the monetary system in this country, from a public system in this country with money issued by the supreme authority of the realm to make possible the distribution and exchange of wealth, to a private system with money or its complete equivalent, issued by private people and created by them to lend at interest.
>
> "These innovations grew up sub rosa and without any definite national sanction, and it is only since the war that it has been impossible any longer to disguise their real character or be blind to the open menace they throw down to all duly constituted law and authority. . . . They are different from the principles of bad or counterfeit money as commonly understood, only in the enormous extent and capriciousness of the money privately uttered.
>
> "During inflation, as occurred at the end of the war, hundreds of millions of pounds are, by these methods, uttered at the direct expense of the other owners of money, to anybody giving evidence of an ability to repay, and willing to pay interest on the pretended loan.
>
> "During deflation, as now, the arteries of the nation are sucked of their life-blood by the deliberate attempt to destroy equally large aggregates of money.
>
> "In light of present knowledge and experience the system appears as high treason against the nation, a monstrous cancer invading its heart."

Later in his book Professor Soddy says: "If some people are to be allowed to issue and destroy money, all the others may as well give up at once any idea of economic independence or freedom, and hire themselves out to those who have this power on the best terms they can. There cannot be two heads in one State and the people have to choose between Parliament and the Banks."

What is behind this bank money is the national credit. The national credit is based upon the national wealth. The national wealth is the property of the people, not of the banks. The only value behind bank money is what the people put there themselves. No more stupid thing has ever been done in the history of the world than to allow private banking companies to turn the national credit into money and hire it out at interest to the people, whose property it was in the first place.

Sweden Adopts Goods Standard Money

Production and Money to keep Step

IT will be news to most New Zealanders to learn that Sweden has put its paper money on a goods standard basis. That is to say, its currency and credit are being regulated by a price index so as to keep prices on a steady level.

This is the most important monetary reform made by any country in the world. Here is the story as told in the October issue of a Swedish financial journal, the "Skandinaviska Kreditaktie-bolaget":—

"Now that the severance from gold has taken place, it would be rather difficult to persuade the general public that it is desirable to return to the gold standard as soon as possible and at any cost. This is primarily due to the realization of the defects inherent in the gold standard system itself, as shown by the experience of recent years. Partly owing to refusal to receive payments in goods, partly because international lending has been abnormally restricted, vast amounts of gold have been accumulated by a few countries. The result has been an artificial demand for gold, which is bound to lead to a fall of prices.

"It may be objected that the prevailing depression is due to other factors, such as injudicious expansion, accumulated stocks of goods, etc. Such objections, however, do not validate the contention that it is urgent to make every possible effort to perfect the monetary system. Such endeavours should aim at maintaining the value of money, as far as possible, constant.

"This aim, of course, can be attained even with a paper currency. The proposals on these lines submitted by several well-known political economists, (e.g., Wicksell and Keynes), the essential feature of which is that the value of money should be regulated according to a price index, are now being tested in practice by the Swedish Riksbank. The latter has made arrangements for the compilation of a price index, covering both wholesale and retail prices, and specially adapted for serving the purpose indicated.

It is noteworthy that the Riksbank has thus set up a definite goal for its monetary policy in the immediate future.

"And as the Swedish national bank has previously succeeded in pursuing a predetermined course of monetary policy with a free paper currency, there is reason to expect that its present endeavours to the same end will meet with success. If similar declarations of policy were made also by other countries with a paper standard, first and foremost by Great Britain this would greatly conduce to clear up the present monetary situation.

"As an alternative to a system of monetary policy on the lines above indicated, we could fall back on the former gold standard. But one can scarcely be accused of indulging in carping criticism of that system, if one expresses the view that it cannot be recommended as the best possible system in all circumstances."

The essential difference between this Swedish currency basis and the gold basis is that on gold currency and credit increase or decrease according to the quantity of gold held by a nation. On the Swedish basis currency and credit must increase as national production increases, otherwise prices will fall.

Under the gold standard people who make two blades of grass to grow where there was but one before depreciate the value of everybody else's blades of grass, lower prices, and make it difficult for all to pay their debts.

Under the Swedish system increased wealth automatically means increased money in circulation. Thus the more of everything produced the better for everybody. Sweden has in Professor Gustav Cassel one of the foremost economists in the world who has repeatedly warned Europe of what this present mad deflation inflicted on the world by the international financial gang must lead to. What Sweden has done New Zealand can do!

John A. Lee

John A. Lee

In New Zealand John A. Lee is remembered with reverence by the Depression era generation, despite his vigorous attacks on the also iconic Michael J. Savage, Labour's first Prime Minster, and finance minister Walter Nash, as sell-outs. As the following three items show, Lee had an extraordinary knowledge of not only the banking system but of those covert workings of history that would today have consigned Lee to ridicule by academia and the news media as "a conspiracy theorist."

The three works by Lee show that during the Depression era the common New Zealander knew a great deal about the banking system and it was discussed intelligently at all levels of society; that the tour of New Zealand by Major C. H. Douglas, formulator of 'Social Credit', had a major influence on political thinking, not only with the establishment of a Social Credit movement, but more particularly with the influence he had within the Labour Party.

Due to the 'third way' character of Social Credit, the Douglas tour also had a seminal impact on the 'Right' with the 20,000 strong New Zealand Legion of Dr. Campbell Begg adopting the Social Credit plan. Lee's pamphlets also show that the election of the First New Zealand Labour Government, a seminal moment in New Zealand's history, was primarily on the basis of the party's platform of nationalising the Reserve Bank, repudiating the debt-finance system, and issuing state credit. It is a forgotten part of New Zealand history, but one of the most important, because it shows what was possible, even with the limited measures that were taken by the Labour Government, one salient, yet buried, example being the state housing project which was funded debt-free by state credit. Despite the fame of New Zealand's state housing, few people, including academics, realise how it was funded. Books on the era, while describing the state housing programme, say nothing of the innovative financial policies that made it possible, while today Labour and National governments are totally ignorant on how to solve current housing problems.

John A. Lee

Born in Dunedin, New Zealand, in 1891 in poor, working class circumstances, John was a bright student, despite his tendency to 'wag' school often. He was also a petty thief at a young age, earning him a sentence to Industrial School, where discipline was tough, but where he became an assistant teacher.

Swaggie and War Hero

Lee next worked as an itinerant farm labourer, becoming a 'swaggie', moving about the country with small groups of jobless men, reading, and becoming politically conscious. He became a socialist of a non-doctrinaire type, finding in the camaraderie of the 'swaggies' the character of social community that should be the norm of a country, the socialism that Australians referred to as ' mateship'. Reaching Auckland in 1913, Lee first heard the oratory of the so-called ' Red Fedders' of the Federation of Labour, including Labour stalwarts such as Peter Fraser, Michael J. Savage, Bob Semple, and Harry Holland. Lee began reading the works of the Fabian socialists, of Syndicalists and of the Syndicalist philosopher George Sorel. He was particularly influenced by the novels of Jack London whose socialism was very unorthodox in its embrace of Nietzsche and the heroic-individualist struggles in raw nature by both man and animal.

Lee enlisted for the Great War in 1916 in contrast to the anti-war stance of the Labour movement. He was noted for his 'fearless gallantry', being awarded the Distinguished Conduct Medal for his capture of a machine gun post. He read socialist tracts while under fire, and as front-line soldiers often do, became contemptuous of the home-front politicians. In 1917 he was invalided home, having lost an arm. He joined the Labour Party, quickly becoming noted as a street orator.

Lee was elected to parliament in 1922, speaking for the veterans. He advocated increased population and a permanent body of efficient instructors who could quickly train citizens in soldiery. Lee's socialism was in particular from the start directed at debt-finance capitalism. He saw nationalisation of banking rather than nationalisation of property as the key. In this regard he opposed the party's policy of land nationalisation, urging instead that the farmer be freed from debt. He wrote 'in this way our proposals would get at the criminals, and not as at present, threaten the victims'. It is an outlook that the Left never has really understood.

In 1925 Lee made 'the financial dictatorship' an election issue. He was a decade ahead of C. H. Douglas' impact on New Zealand. New Zealand could be insulated against the booms and busts manipulated by international finance. This could end the criminal folly of 'poverty amidst plenty', which several years later was to see many states throughout the world paying farmers to destroy crops and livestock to maintain price levels, while people went hungry, because there was not enough 'money' in circulation. Lee rejected free trade, which many socialists even then supported, and advocated a protected economy. He saw the danger of attempting to compete with 'backward countries' and preferred high priced local goods than competing against the 'rice standard' of coolie labour. Credit would have to be regulated by the state, not the banks. Secondary industry would increase employment, which would allow for an increase in population, which in turn would increase the home market, and enable rising wages. The perquisite for establishing this national economic system would be 'a centralised and controlled exchange system and a state bank to issue state credit'. However, many in the Labour Party hierarchy regarded Lee's proposals as a departure from doctrinaire socialism. Walter Nash in particular, who would become minister of finance in the First Labour Government, opposed detachment of New Zealand from the Bank of England and what Lee referred to as Britain's 'shylockcracy'. Lee stated to the 1933 Labour caucus, 'One would think that money was a heavenly manna and that we had to starve until we had a heavenly miracle'.

First Labour Government

Thanks largely to Lee's efforts, Labour went into the 1935 General Election with a policy of establishing a 'central credit authority', stating that private credit creation 'thwarts the will of government'. As Lee stated in the following pamphlets, Labour was elected to office on the promise of banking reform. Prime Minister Savage offered Lee a meaningless position as under-secretary to the Prime Minister. After pressure from Cabinet, Lee was appointed under-secretary of housing, amounting to ministerial responsibility. Despite Labour's election promises on banking, Lee had to fight hard to get credit for state housing, but by 1937 the programme was well underway.

It was to push Labour into fulfilling its election promises on banking and credit that Lee published his pamphlet *Money Power for the People* in 1937, analysing Labour's 'promises, performances, and future'. The appointment of Tim Armstrong as Minster of Housing in 1938 was a snub at Lee, to which he responded by circulating members of Caucus with an attack on Walter Nash's financial policies. As one might expect, the push for Lee's expulsion from the Labour Party came from the Communist faction that then dominated the Federation of Labour. Lee not only saw the control of banking rather than nationalisation of property as essential to the creation of the ' new labour state', but regarded the trades unions as having a social purpose, rather than as instruments of class struggle.

Democratic Labour Party

In April 1939 Lee wrote a critique of the 'indecision' of the Labour Caucus entitled, *A letter which every New Zealander should read*, addressed 'to all members of the Parliamentary Labour Party'. In January 1940 Lee was expelled from the party for his criticism of Michael Savage, who died three days later. Two month's later he founded the Democratic Labour Party, decimating many branches of the Labour Party as the grass roots went over to Lee. He attacked both the 'union gangsters' and the 'money power'.

A by-election in 1943 saw the Labour and Communist parties align to resist Democratic Labour, however the DLP candidate got a strong showing of 26.7%. The party's name was changed to the Democratic Soldier Labour Party, to give servicemen 'a chance to help build a new order'. This also highlighted Lee's long-time criticism of the pacifist record of Labour politicians during World War I. The DSLP contested 54 seats in the 1943 General Election with over half being servicemen or veterans, on a platform of debt-free credit, worker co-management, and the recall of the African Division. The Communists were vitriolic in their opposition, condemning Lee as 'aping the Fascists', and accusing him of the 'militarisation of politics'. The party polled 23.29% and did particularly well among soldiers, but Lee lost his Grey Lynn seat.

The party declined, and Lee set on a road as an acclaimed novelist, while continuing with his newspaper, *John A. Lee's Weekly*. He condemned the post-war international financial system established by Bretton Woods, that created the World Bank and International Monetary Fund, which he said was to 'make the world safe for the money lenders'. Lee died in 1982, esteemed for his contributions to New Zealand literature, while the crucial issue of banking and credit is today forgotten by the 'more educated' generations. The following three articles—*"Money Power for the People"* (1937), *"A Letter which Every New Zealander Should Read"* (1939), and *"This Debt Slavery"* (1940) are, I believe, among the most cogent arguments for banking reform ever written.

Money Power for the People

At the last General Election the Labour Party promised much in regard to monetary reform. Today there is criticism that Labour has achieved little. In this pamphlet will be found the record of what Labour promised and the nature of the magnificent foundation which Labour has established. No democratic Government has ever advanced so fast or so far in the world of money policy, and certainly no possible alternative Government is likely to go further.

When discussing the future, the author of the pamphlet sets out to express only his own personal opinion and is alone responsible for the views expressed, although the views coincide with Labour's promises.

The pamphlet is dedicated to that earnest body of men and women whose good fellowship has made the Grey Lynn Branch of the Party so successful.

—John A. Lee, 1937.

Banking and the New Zealand Labour Government

The world-wide depression, side by side with a glut of commodities and a slowing-down of industry, caused: banking and money policy, that most important of all capitalistic monopolies, to be scrutinised very carefully, prior to last election. If the world, and if New Zealand as part of the world, during 1931-35 had become intensely conscious of the great part an intelligent money system must play in a policy of reconstruction, the Labour Party in New Zealand had played their part in having that awareness of monetary factors and their relationship to depression made known to the people. Hundreds of meetings, of a size never achieved prior to 1931, were held from end to end of New Zealand. The mind and voice of everyone seemed to be concentrated on money. On street corner or tram, in the sitting room or at the sale-

John A. Lee

yard, at the dairy factory of a morning — wherever and whenever people gathered there was discussion about banking and money.

The New Zealand Labour Party has always had as an important plank of its political programme the complete State ownership and control of the machinery of currency and credit, and this plank has been emphasised over the years. But during the great depression, in which deflation succeeded under-consumption, the interest of the community in money became all-absorbing. Money policy is a political high explosive, as likely to disintegrate a party's following as the political enemy, but the time had grown opportune to amplify Labour's statement of monetary policy and to stress the importance of control of the monetary factor as an aid to a distributive system based on Socialism.

On the 17th April, 1933, a Conference of the New Zealand Labour Party had before it the report of a committee which had been set up to amplify the Party's banking and money policy. The committee reported on the relationship of banking to Labour's proposals. The committee's report was adopted unanimously by Conference, and from that moment the Labour Party was pledged to make complete control of the nation's financial machinery, not a portion, but the first portion of its legislative and administrative policy.

In New Zealand, Labour had not had any period of tenure in office as a Government and had been able to study from evidence the reason for many of the disastrous failures of well-intentioned Labour Parties in other countries. In nearly every country disastrous failure had been brought about by Labour failing to acquire immediately complete financial power. In Great Britain, Labour Governments had been allowed to exist by forces opposed to Labour Government as long as those Governments had been content to tinker only with wages and hours, making a shilling increase in this or a shilling reduction on that, the while avoiding any attempt to alter fundamentally the nature of the capitalist structure.

An end is soon reached to the capacity of government within the capitalist system to tinker with wages and hours. Profit systems, and particularly in partially free trade communities, find their capacity to adjust industry to the human factor determined all the time by the cost of competing goods produced by humans in other lands. Sweeping changes can be effected only by repeatedly and continually breaking down the profit-making system.

Opposing the Money Lenders

When any British Labour Government has been confronted with the necessity of making a revolutionary change in banking machinery, the entrenched financial powers have been strong enough to disrupt that Government and to bring it to its knees. Looking across the Tasman to Australia, New Zealand Labour had seen a Labour Government — and a good Government — returned to office and allowed to carry out a certain amount of Labour policy; but because that Government had tactlessly neglected important banking legislation until progress without that legislation became impossible, the Government of Labour was defeated and subsequently thrown from office.

There is a Golden Age of Government wherein it should attempt to make the fundamental changes that are necessary to its administrative continuance in office. That age is after the hour of victory and before an electorate grows sceptical and disillusioned at unfulfilled promises. Labour in New Zealand saw the few gentlemen who controlled the Board of the Commonwealth Bank of Australia nationally-owned bank, the control of which had been surrendered to a few private individuals — exercise for a vital moment in Australia's history the same power to defeat the elected Government that is being regularly exercised by the Supreme Court in the United States of America, except that whereas the Supreme Court of the United States bases its sovereignty on what it calls the Constitution — the Constitution varying sometimes with, the state of a Judge's liver — the Commonwealth Bank Board based all its activities on what it was pleased to call sound finance." In a word, Labour being Socialist and wanting to base money policy on human well-being instead of on Capitalist profit, had to be outlawed by Capitalist directors. As this article is being dictated, the Board of the Commonwealth Bank of Australia has again swaggered and bullied and has threatened Australia that except that Prime Ministers of the various Australian States refrain from criticism of the Commonwealth Bank Board and adopt a "meek and humble" attitude, the Commonwealth Bank might refuse to underwrite State loans. Meanwhile Labour in New Zealand underwrites at 3 and a quarter percent as against Australia's 4%.

With example after example of defeat to profit by, the Labour Party in New Zealand, convinced that no improvement in social conditions could be effected permanently without complete control of financial power, was determined to win that power in the golden moment of victory. While the public were still acclaiming Labour's advent and were anxious for Labour to control finance, Labour intended to use that goodwill, knowing that if any unfair obstruction was placed in Labour's way, an immediate appeal to the people would yield a striking endorsement. This sort of tactic should be the unvarying tactic of democratically elected Labour. To win the main citadel in the moment of enthusiasm is easy.

Hence it was that the Labour Conference in April, 1933, amplified the New Zealand Labour Party's financial policy and placed that financial policy right in the forefront of the programme so that a democratic mandate should be won for the plan.

Reporting to Conference on the 17th April, the Committee prefaced their policy statement with a preamble, in connection with which all the machinery proposals were to be read. I reproduce below the whole preamble:—

Preamble

"**The Purpose of Production:** The purpose of all production, primary and secondary, is to supply the social and economic requirements of the people and the duty of the State is to organise productive and distributive agencies in order to utilise the natural resources for this purpose.

"Only a courageous and vigorous policy can save our country. The policy of deflation has been pursued to such an extent that even if there were an equitable distribution of existing income it would not be sufficient to allow thousands of householders, farmers and businessmen to become solvent. A policy must start either from a foundation of wholesale repudiation and bankruptcy or else we must organise the development of industry and extend the social services to increase the income of the people so as to provide an adequate standard of living and enable them to meet their present commitments. The chaotic state of the world has already reduced prices of exports to ruinous levels, and our present economic position is, to a large extent, due to the fact that New Zealand currency and credit is determined by overseas price levels.

"**Credit Basis:** Overseas prices and conditions cannot any longer be allowed to dictate New Zealand's living standards. By proper planning of production, with control of marketing and finance, New Zealand can establish her own living standard. The basis of all credit and currency must be production (goods and services)."

"This basis can only be established and maintained by expanding the incomes of the mass of the people in accord with production and their social and economic requirements.

"Equities in land and homes which have been endangered by the deflationary policy of the Government should be re-established on the basis of an average of wholesale prices ruling during the past seven years. Present occupiers of land and homes must be safeguarded against foreclosure pending the stabilisation of internal prices on a basis which will allow them to meet their commitments.

"**Unemployment:** The workers today unemployed are our fellow citizens who are out of work through no fault of their own. They are entitled to employment at a living wage. Failing such employment, they should be paid a sustenance wage sufficient to provide the necessaries of life for them and their dependants. The conditions and pay of the men on relief works are a standing disgrace to the Dominion. The existing degrading system should be abolished at the earliest possible moment. The Party will organise productive development work for all who are able to do it, including present relief workers, unemployed women and the youths who are leaving our schools. Pending organisation of employment, the Party will immediately increase the present rates of pay for relief work."

"**Guaranteed Prices:** Organised employment in primary and secondary industries, with a vigorous public works policy, local and national, at wages and salaries based on national production, will ensure to the farmer on the land, the worker in industry, and all others who render social service, an income that will maintain a standard of living to which the people of the Dominion are entitled. The ruinous policy of deflation and bankruptcy has been consistently opposed by the Labour Movement, and we affirm that a complete reversal of the Government's policy and the economic management of the country generally has become a necessity of the first magnitude."

Following upon the preamble, there appeared a series of nine points setting out in the barest possible language the lines along which the Government would legislate to give effect to the intentions of the preamble. The points were as follows:-

John A. Lee

1. Immediate control by the State of the entire banking system. The State to be the sole authority for the issue of credit and currency. Provision of credit and currency to ensure production and distribution of the commodities which are required and which can be economically produced in the Dominion, with guaranteed prices, wages and salaries.

2. Conservation of present holders' interests in land and homes by readjustment of all mortgages on a basis of average prices for the past seven years.

3. Guaranteed prices for primary products. Negotiated agreements with Great Britain and other countries for marketing of primary products, with reciprocal contracts for the import of those classes of commodities which cannot be economically produced in the Dominion.

4. Promotion of agreements between the various control boards, other associations of primary producers, and distributors' and consumers' organisations to ensure orderly marketing at guaranteed prices of the primary products required for consumption in the Dominion.

5. Fostering of secondary industries so as to ensure the production of those commodities which can be economically produced in the Dominion, thus providing employment for our own people, with the resultant increase in the internal demand for our primary and secondary products, with less dependency on the fluctuating and glutted overseas markets.

6. Organisation of productive and development work on the following lines: Land development and settlement; completion of necessary public works; construction of backblocks roads; secondary and main highways; assistance to local authorities to undertake approved works; financial assistance in the development of secondary industries.

7. (a) Utilisation of mechanical inventions, new processes, and research knowledge, (b) Immediate reduction in the hours of labour, in order to employ a greater number of workers in industry to meet the displacement of labour by machinery, (c) Guaranteed wages and salaries in accord with national production.

8. Negotiation with British Government and overseas financial houses for the purpose of covering the overseas debt to a lower rate of interest, and readjustment to price levels operating at time of raising loans.

9. Negotiations with British Government for the purpose of reducing the principal and interest of war debt, or its cancellation.

The preamble and the poiicy were used as the basis for much explanatory memoranda and pamphlets, which were circulated by the tens of thousands.

The Douglas Credit Party was also, at that time, interesting the people of New Zealand in credit and currency reform, Douglas Credit agitation sweeping New Zealand like a religious revival. While no one could outline any Douglas Credit constructive proposals, nearly everyone was able to understand and agree with the Douglas Credit movement's criticism of the orthodox financial machine.

The very difficulty of understanding Douglas and his algebraic symbols and theorems rendered Conservatives more willing to listen to the Douglas movement's critical and able analysis of capitalist finance. Thousands who because of past political hostility found the Labour Party altogether too vulgar an organisation, rallied to the Douglas Credit Movement, which in a few months reached extraordinary proportions and sold a huge amount of literature. These thousands, after being won to a position of scepticism in regard to Capitalist finance, could not rest in the Douglas Movement but started to study the practical and positive proposals of the New Zealand Labour Party. And although the Douglas Credit Movement withered away almost as rapidly as it had blossomed, nevertheless it can be said finally that the Douglas Credit Movement's activities were the corridor through which tens of thousands of voters entered the Labour Party. Douglas Credit agitation must have a big share of the credit for any Labour success, although the Labour Party is thoroughly Socialist in its policy.

The idea that bank credit should be used to enable people to consume goods which were in abundance but which could not circulate during the depression under the Capitalist profit system, and that bank credit should be based on goods and services rather than merely used to maintain the production of goods at a Capitalist profit, definitely captured New Zealand. The opponents of Labour in New

John A. Lee

Zealand, including the whole of the New Zealand daily press, with the exception of one small-town Labour journal, were constant in their vituperative criticism. The Forbes-Coates Party, which had become the most unpopular Government New Zealand had ever known, lost no opportunity to debate the Labour Party's policy, drawing pictures of a Labour Government's credit inflation producing the catastrophic results that were associated with the collapse of the mark in Germany. The lead given by Snowden and the Conservatives in England, who intimated Post Office Savings Bank depositors with the threat that Labour Party policy meant the confiscation of Post Office deposits, was utilised in New Zealand, where for a couple of decades it had been an anti-Labour device. The banks which, no doubt, had always privately contributed to the political funds of the anti-Labour Parties, came into the open during the period leading up to the election and during the election, advertising extensively in the daily press the merits of "sound finance."

Under no circumstances can it be represented that the people of New Zealand did not understand that for which they were voting. The one question dealt with most extensively in all candidates' speeches, both in industrial and rural areas, was finance. Everyone emphasised the necessity of commencing the Labour Party's programme by taking complete control of the banking machinery.

Despite a press that was as unanimous as it was bitterly hostile, Labour won through to a crashing victory. The moment the victory had been achieved the press, which had a few days earlier been drawing attention to the extreme and dangerous nature of Labour's proposals, started to engage in widespread publicity appreciative of the moderation of certain Labour men who had been elected — an old habit. In particular, the press found it possible to repeat many nice things about the Hon, Mr. Nash, although as we near election again press opinion is veering to its traditional attitude. The prophesied run on the Post Office Savings Bank did not take place, and maybe it was thought that it was better to humour Labour and counsel moderation at the moment of victory than to continue with the policy of antagonism. Besides, the temper of the country, following upon the election, was such that the policy of "giving Labour a fair show" was good newspaper policy, and there is too a subtle psychological influence upon certain minds in counsels of moderation.

The caucus of the Labour Party met, Cabinet was selected, and certain committees were set up to prepare legislation for the first session

Opposing the Money Lenders

of Parliament. The Party again reaffirmed its intention of winning complete financial power as the first move toward a new social order. Following the General Election, the banking interests were in such a chastened mood that they probably would have been willing to guarantee the supply of all funds necessary for the maintenance of Labour Government, and of popular Labour Government, at a very low rate of interest and for very long terms, as an alternative to the Labour Party's policy. It may be that such offers were privately made. If they were, the Labour Government, with the destruction of other Governments that had relied on the goodwill of their enemies in mind, had no intention of falling into traps of this sort, and were determined to win power.

Parliament met in March, 1936. The Labour Government had already done much administratively to improve the lot of unemployed workers, but every administrative Act that had the effect of sending up expenditure rendered still more inevitable the passage of banking legislation. Pass, banking legislation must, and pass early.

While the first important Bill presented to the House was the Government Railways Amendment Bill, a Bill which restored control of the Government Railways from a nominated Board free of political influence to a responsible Minister, the only reason why the Reserve Bank of New Zealand Amendment Bill was not the first to be passed was that it could not be got ready for the opening days of the session. However, there was little delay for by the 3rd April the Reserve Bank of New Zealand Amendment Bill was ready for its second reading.

A Central Reserve Bank, with sole right of note issue, had been set up by the Forbes-Coates administration in the year 1933. The Central Reserve Bank then established was a semi-public institution, the shares being held by both private shareholders and by the Government of the day, the directors being elected by private shareholders and nominated by the State. The bank was in a position of complete independence, although no doubt the board, which was appointed by the Forbes-Coates Government, felt bound to give effect to Government policy. However, there was no Governmental power to check the board in the exercise of complete freedom.

The Reserve Bank of New Zealand Amendment Bill of 1936 was revolutionary in the amendments and additions it effected to the Reserve Bank Act. The Reserve Bank of New Zealand Amendment Bill commenced by making the bank a complete State institution, the private shareholders being bought out at a handsome profit to shareholders. The Board of Directors of the Reserve Bank was completely reconstituted. Whereas under the original Act the board was elective and there was no provision for retirement except for bankruptcy or mental inefficiency, the New Act provided that: —

"(1) The ordinary members of the Board of Directors in office on the commencement of this Act shall continue to be members of that board, and shall thereafter hold office during the pleasure of the Governor-General in Council:

Provided that, unless they sooner vacate their respective offices, they shall retire in accordance with the following provisions, namely:—

(a) Two shall retire on the thirty-first day of July, nineteen hundred and thirty-six;

(b) One shall retire on the thirty-first day of July, nineteen hundred and thirty-seven;

(c) Two shall retire on the thirty-first day of July, nineteen hundred and thirty-eight;

(d) One shall retire on the thirty-first day of July, nineteen hundred and thirty-nine;

(e) One shall retire on the thirty-first day of July, nineteen hundred and forty;

(2) The members so to retire in any year shall be determined by the board by ballot.

(3) If any ordinary member of the board in office on the commencement of this Act vacates his office otherwise than by retirement in accordance with the provisions of subsection one of this section, the Governor-General in Council may appoint some person in his stead, to hold office on the same terms as his predecessor in office. The provisions of this subsection shall apply in the event of any person appointed under this subsection vacating his office otherwise than by retirement in accordance with the foregoing provisions of this section.

(4) The distinction between State directors and shareholders' directors is hereby abolished.'

In other words, a period was set for the maximum tenure of office, but the Government of the day, by Order in Council, acquired power to compel the retirement of any director at any time. Power was also taken to ensure that only the directors the Government wanted should be appointed. Today the Board of Directors is the direct servant of the Government of the day, and must give effect to the policy of the Government of the day or the board can be removed or altered at will.

There was a re-statement of the general function of the Reserve Bank as follows;—

(1) It shall be the general function of the Reserve Bank within the limits of its powers, to give effect as far as may be to the monetary policy of the Government, as communicated to it from time to time by the Minister of Finance. For this purpose and to the end that the economic and social welfare of New Zealand may be promoted and maintained, the bank shall regulate and control credit and currency in New Zealand, the transfer of moneys to or from the sale of any New Zealand products and for the time being are held overseas.

(2) For the purpose of enabling the Reserve Bank to fulfil its functions the Governor-General may by Order in Council make all such regulations, not inconsistent with the principal Act or this Act, as he from time to time considers necessary, and may prescribe therein such penalties as he thinks fit for the breach of any such regulations, not exceeding in any case a fine of one thousand pounds for any offence, or, in the case of a continuing offence, not exceeding a fine of five hundred pounds for every day on which the offence is committed or continued.

(3) All regulations made under the authority of this section shall be laid before Parliament within twenty-eight days after the making thereof if Parliament then in session, and if not, then within twenty-eight days after the commencement of the next ensuing session thereof.

(4) This section is in substitution for section twelve of the principal Act, and that section is hereby accordingly repealed.

The bank was given increased power to discount bills. The bank was also authorised to grant accommodation by way of overdraft for the purchase and marketing of New Zealand produce, which is, of course, the clause under which the Guaranteed Price Scheme for dairy produce is at present being financed. Authority was given to the Reserve Bank to buy and sell Government securities. Clause 14 of the new Act, a clause of vital importance, compelled the Reserve Bank, under Government direction, to undertake the underwriting of any loan which the Government desired to raise, the wording being as follows:—

> "By authority of the Governor-General in Council, underwrite any loan proposed to be raised by the New Zealand Government,"

In the terms of the original Act it was unlawful for the Reserve Bank to underwrite any such loan.

The Act was amended to increase the authority of the Reserve Bank to grant temporary accommodation to the Treasury, the Treasury being empowered to borrow from the Reserve Bank the complete amount of the revenue or estimated revenue for the year

In terms of the original Act, the Reserve Bank was given complete control over the ownership of sterling exchange (London Funds) subject to the necessity of making exchange available, under certain conditions, on demand.

The Labour Government acquired power under the amending legislation to cause the bank to completely suspend the right of anyone to demand sterling exchange on the direction of the Minister of Finance. This power is of vital importance as it arms the Government with power to control those international movements of gangster finance capital that can occur in times of political emergency and that can do grave harm to a country's industries, that can raid a country's external credit.

The Secretary to the Treasury, who is a member of the Board of the Reserve Bank, was given the right to vote at all meetings of the board.

Subsection 3 of Clause 18 of the Bill gave the Government, by Order in Council, power to remove the Governor or the Deputy-Governor during his term of office if he became permanently incapable of performing the duties of his office; under the clause there can be no doubt but that Cabinet is the sole judge of what constitutes permanent incapacity. Another clause gave the Minister of Finance power to appoint an Acting Governor or Acting Deputy Governor.

It was provided that an annual report of the operations of the Reserve Bank of New Zealand should be laid before Parliament so that the people's elected representatives may discuss the people's bank.

Under Section 45 of the principal Act of 1933 provision was made for the trading banks to lodge balances with the Reserve Bank to the extent of 3 per cent, of their time liabilities and 7 per cent, of their demand liabilities. Clause 2 of the amending Act gave the Minister of Finance power to cause, by notice published in the Gazette, the Governor of the bank to vary upward or downward the balance required to be maintained by any bank. This power enables the Minister of Finance to check inflation by causing trading banks to deposit a greater proportion of their time and demand liabilities, and this power also arms the Minister with authority which effectively enables him to resist any efforts on the part of trading banks to raid London Funds by compelling the Trading Banks to maintain such New Zealand balances as the Minister thinks fit.

An additional clause was added to the Act under which the Trading Banks were compelled to disclose the "aggregate of the unexercised overdraft authorities of customers" so that potential as well as actual purchasing power might be estimated from period to period and so that the curtailing or expansionist activities of Trading Banks could be adequately gauged.

Of course, after winning financial power the best clause in the Reserve Bank Bill is the Clause under which the profits gained through use of the power return to the nation.

Banking Progress To Date.

The new powers conferred upon the Government by the Reserve Bank of New Zealand Amendment Bill have been used with a good deal of caution in the past eleven months, some think with too much caution, others with too little. Certain of the bank's powers have been used from the moment of the bank's establishment. These are the powers that conform to orthodox practice. For instance, the Reserve Bank took over the gold reserve of the associated banks in New Zealand at the moment of the establishment of the Reserve Bank, thereby netting for the Government a handsome profit which represented the difference between the currency value of gold, if the banks had been compelled to redeem their notes, and the commodity value of gold in London. In this way the bank was enabled to commence by securing for New Zealand a very handsome profit. The bank has also become the keeper of the Government's banking accounts, and in addition has taken over the management of the New Zealand national debt. The sole right of note issue was of necessity put into operation almost coincidentally with the establishment of the bank.

Dairy Industry Account:

But the new unorthodox powers are only starting to be used. For instance, the bank is compelled to grant overdraft accommodation to the Dairy Industry Account in such quantity and upon such terms as the Government may direct.

With the establishment of the guaranteed price scheme, the New Zealand Government becomes the owner of all dairy factories avoid paying away large sums in interest to private banks for the advances they were in the habit of receiving an overdraft for unsold produce in store or on the private banks for the advances they were in the habit of receiving on overdraft for unsold produce in store or on the water. Since the State is owner of the produce from the point of shipment until the point at which it is sold to the distributor in Great Britain there are tremendous advantages to the nation in financing with the Reserve Bank, the charges for overdraft accommodation being kept at a minimum, and the profits of the overdraft earned for the National Accounts.

Advances to the Dairy Industry Account fluctuate from day to day as produce is shipped and sold, but at the close of business on April 19, 1937, dairy industry advances amounted to £6,146,667. It would be scarcely accurate to describe this advance as the creation of new money. The private trading banks have in the past granted this accommodation and have profited handsomely by doing so. The Reserve Bank's advances would be just about equivalent to those made by the private banks to finance dairy produce sales in other years, but the community is issuing its own credit and the profit (if any) accruing to the bank for the use of such credit will be remitted to the Consolidated Fund. The probability is that eventually the cost for overdraft accommodation to the Dairy Industry Account will be reduced to a figure sufficient to cover bare accountancy costs. Here, then, is a direct transference of money issuing authority under which £6,146,667 has been temporarily issued from the State Office instead of from private banking interests.

It can be readily seen that if other primary products were also incorporated within a guaranteed scheme the State issued overdraft for marketing would swell tremendously to the private banker's disadvantage. On every penny-piece of the overdraft issue there is the assurance that credit is being made available for the benefit of all of the people and not for the purpose of bringing profits to a few private banking interests. And the State, as a financier of the Dairy Industry Account, has a different attitude to the advance from that of the private banker. The private banker is not concerned with the price at which the commodity upon which he has granted accommodation sells, provided he recoups the advance. The State, having guaranteed a minimum price for butter in New Zealand currency, has a definite interest in using the overdraft accommodation of the Reserve Bank to enable marketing to be orderly, regulated, and at the best possible price that can be acquired from the British market. Thus at the moment under orderly marketing New Zealand butter commands a premium on Danish. In all probability there will be a deficit in the Dairy Industry Account at the end of the year owing to the New Zealand f.o.b. guaranteed price being in advance of the London price for butter, and this deficit only will represent the real credit inflation on account of our dairy production, an inflation of credit based on internal price stability.

Ownership and Control of Sterling Exchange:

In the terms of the Act the Reserve Bank of New Zealand owns all London exchange and under certain circumstances may absolutely refuse such London exchange to anyone. This power to refuse London Funds is a necessary power and allows an opportunity for the bank to be used at a later date for the purpose of a planned economy in New Zealand. The attitude of trading banks to the sale of exchange is that of a Capitalist economy without regard to national considerations. All the banker is concerned about when selling London exchange is whether his client is of good financial standing, and whether an overdraft granted against imports is a transaction on which the banker's client is likely to earn a profit. It may happen that exchange may be sold for transactions, which would be exceedingly profitable in themselves to the bank, and the client and which would yet result in the importation of goods that would completely dislocate New

John A. Lee

Zealand's economy. While at the present moment the bank is selling exchange freely in the manner of all capitalistic banking institutions a day may arrive when Governments will seek to assist New Zealand industry and maybe assist the industry of Great Britain or any country with which New Zealand has an exchange balance, through a more careful scrutiny of the use to which external funds are put. At the present moment the power to refuse exchange is not being utilised and there appears to be no immediate likelihood of its use, short of an attempt by gangster finance to raid London funds. New Zealand has substantial London balances and large quantities of butter are being regularly cleared, and, although the price is not high, it has topped its great competitor for the first time in years. Thanks to the armament scare in Europe and the industrial recovery in America, New Zealand wool has attained an exceptionally high price and mutton and lamb and other meat products are bringing in a fine return.

On March 30, 1936, the sterling exchange available in London to the Government amounted to £24,830,101—a very handsome inheritance for a Labour Government desiring to carry through a policy calculated to bring New Zealand into conflict with international banking hostility. About £3,000,000 worth of New Zealand stock has been redeemed in Great Britain, thereby reducing the external public debt and saving a very large amount of interest to the Public Accounts. Notwithstanding this redemption on April 19, 1937, the London exchange funds amounted to £19,622,337—a very fine position for a Labour Government threatened with such alarmist attacks as have occurred during the past few days in the *"Evening News"* in London, attacks which render it the more necessary to keep London funds high to safeguard New Zealand against privately-controlled gangster capital.

Since, obviously, the Dairy Industry Account advance of over £6,000,000 must represent produce which will be sold in Great Britain this season, the London assets, including cash and goods, must be almost as large as they were twelve months ago, notwithstanding the increased New Zealand demand for British imports consequent upon our high wages. The overseas assets in respect of New Zealand business held by the ordinary trading banks in London and elsewhere, amount to no less a sum than £16,000,000. No doubt the bulk of this is held by the Bank of New Zealand, a semi-State bank on which the Government has four of the six directors, so that the present Labour Government is in an exceptionally fine position to resist any effort to do harm to its financial status in London. Added to this accumulated external surplus there is the fortunate circumstance that no loan obligations are falling due in Great Britain in the immediate future.

If the Hon. Mr. Nash negotiates a reciprocal trading agreement with Great Britain or with any other country, the power to own and control sterling exchange will be of exceptional value. Certainly, while New Zealand has such a large sterling surplus as it now has in London, with regular reductions of London loan indebtedness occurring periodically, only a fool would allow himself to be stampeded by political hostility into selling New Zealand securities at less than their face value. And wise men will give New Zealand, which wants to pay, a fair share of the markets to enable New Zealand to pay, for if Capitalist debt is orthodoxy, it is well to remember that there are a lot of financial heretics in New Zealand.

In addition to the sterling assets, the Reserve Bank has close on £3,000,000 in a gold reserve (currency values only) immediately available to resist any anti-Labour raid. The control and ownership of large sums of London exchange must have been a contributing factor to the success of the New Zealand Government's conversion loan of £4,000,000 in London last year. The conversion was of 6 per cent stock and the new loan was floated at 3 per cent, the total saving in interest to the country being appreciable.

Underwriting: The Reserve Bank is authorised to underwrite New Zealand's loan scrip and has already conducted successful flotations. The Minister of Finance fixes the rate of interest and the Bank must sell or issue stock accordingly. Twelve million pounds worth of monies falling due in New Zealand have been re-converted at a rate of 3 and a half per cent, as against a prior 6 per cent, and at the present moment a loan of £7,000,000 at 3 and a quarter per cent, has been underwritten with the Reserve Bank and is open for public subscription. Investments, no doubt being the unallotted portion of loan issues to date taken up by the Central Reserve Bank, appear in the weekly statement of assets and liabilities of the Reserve Bank of April 19, 1937, at £2,906,450. The conversions arranged have no doubt been very largely subscribed for out of balances and investment surpluses in the accounts of Government Departments. There can be no doubt but that many people believe that the loan falling due should have been taken over completely by the Reserve Bank at due date rather than converted at the lower rate. But the fact that the rate of interest was handsomely reduced by the underwriting of the Central Reserve Bank from 6 per cent, to 3 and a half per cent, was in itself a decided advantage to the people of New Zealand. Nevertheless, the operation was merely orthodox Capitalist finance at a lower rate of interest and it is interesting to appreciate that the British Government without financial power have just raised a defence loan at 2 and a half per cent. I believe that the Labour Party looks toward the day when the complete refinancing of loans falling due will be performed by the Central Reserve Bank and that the Bank will not merely act as agent for funds borrowed from private individuals. Short of some such action the debt will be compounded forever. If there is to be any interest on public finance a Labour Government must secure that interest for the people. Given time, the Reserve Bank must and will arrange our finance, or at some future date the Capitalist bailiff will liquidate New Zealand's social experiment.

A new loan of £7,000,000 to provide funds for the State Advances Corporation is now being raised at a 3 and a quarter per cent rate. How much of the loan will be subscribed by the public and trading banks, insurance companies, etc., and how much will be left to be taken up by the New Zealand Reserve Bank, cannot be stated until the loan closes. A considerable number of people would hope to quote one Labour member "that not half a crown is subscribed." Certainly I want to see the new powers utilised to the maximum. Personally, I should like to see every conversion or new loan underwritten at a rate too low for Capitalist subscription.

It is interesting to notice that on October 28, 1935, investments, which would include stock held by the Reserve Bank amounted to £1,529,987. As at October 26, 1936 investments amounted to £2,186,244. In the statement of the Central Reserve Bank issued on April 19, 1937, investments are taken into account at £2,906,450, so that an increasing quantity of scrip is being held by the Central Reserve Bank, but the scrip is negotiable and a good deal may be held only temporarily!'

The power to secure funds at a reasonable rate of interest, or, indeed, at the cost of bookkeeping, is necessary to a Labour Government attempting to introduce a new policy. Not to borrow privately for public purposes is Labour policy as I see it. A few days ago, when the Board of the Commonwealth Bank of Australia was publicly questioned regarding the necessity of underwriting a loan at a low rate of interest for the various Australian State Government's the chairman of the Board of Control said that his board had no intention of interfering with what he called "the market rate for money." In a word, the sovereign powers of the State were handed over to the

Opposing the Money Lenders

Associated Banks, who fix the market rate notwithstanding that the Commonwealth is a Government Bank. When the Premiers of Australian States criticised the Commonwealth Bank Board for their unwillingness to make credit available in sufficient quantity and at a reasonable rate, the chairman of the bank issued a public statement to the effect that the Commonwealth Bank would not make the funds available at all if the Australian Premiers did not refrain from public criticism. This most extraordinary attitude shows to what extent Capitalist finance can dictate the policy of Governments who represent only the people. In New Zealand the Minister can fix the rate.

New Issues: Although the power to underwrite and arrange fresh borrowings has been availed of rather than the power to make new issues, except where the issue is an overdraft, such as has been arranged for the Dairy Industry Account, one definite issue has been arranged for. The Government has instructed the Reserve Bank to make £5,000,000 worth of credit available for housing purposes. These funds will be drawn upon by the Housing Account of the State Advances Corporation. All the funds so advanced will be used to create new assets in the form of houses and a straight-out issue of money for the creation of such assets was considered justifiable. The instruction to the Reserve Bank, according to the Hon. Mr. Nash's statement to Parliament, specifically prohibits the Reserve Bank from negotiating the sale of any portion of this issue, so that the whole issue is to be new money upon which the interest earned will belong in its entirety to the State. And the houses, of course, will belong to the State. Five million pounds is available through a Housing Department and to the Local Bodies of New Zealand for the purpose of building houses. This is very definitely a radical use of the new powers conferred on the Government by legislation.

It will be noted that in no way has there been an issue for the purpose of meeting current expenditure except to guarantee dairy produce stability, but that the issue has been made only for the purpose of creating permanent assets. This principle of the State issuing money for the purpose of constructing assets and thus saving the cost of the interest and sinking fund charges to the community, should be applied at as early a date as possible to the financing of the construction of schools, hospitals and public buildings of all sorts. To the writer, this sort of State issue should be extended to every field where an advance will utilise idle labour and raw materials. Such advances should be made against the production of goods, whether the goods be houses, bridges, schools or hospitals. The food and clothing for such idle labour is already being found today in New Zealand and the additional goods produced will be equal to any advance if advances are made with care. Nor is there any reason why the State should pay interest when making an advance against the annual production or manufacture of any form of consumption goods such as butter, meat, boots, furniture. If production is planned the advance will be based on the production of goods certain to be consumed and worth the advance. This is what occurs under the Capitalist overdraft system.

What sanctifies the Capitalist overdraft process is the Capitalist profit which is believed to free advances from inflationary evils contained in a Socialist advance concerned only with the production of consumables. By using idle labour, the State will have increased wealth that it cannot have under the profit system. True, the increased circulation may set up a demand for imports rather than for the additional income produced in New Zealand, but is fear of exchange control to keep us permanently poorer? While a rate of interest to cover extravagances in planning is wise, the interest should be payable always to the State, except that one believes that Capitalism is the best of all possible systems. To the extent that hydro-electrification is a New Zealand-made job, and we have idle men and raw materials or capacity to produce raw materials, it would be reasonable to finance such an undertaking with an issue from a Reserve Bank, although in the event of there not being sufficient London exchange available to secure the necessary machinery, which is not made in New Zealand, external borrowing could be justified for the purpose of completing the job. We are paying to keep men idle frequently. The additional production would recoup the cost of keeping them employed. But then, as the Prime Minister has promised, we should be basing production on goods and services, not on financial profit.

Consumption Goods: The one great danger about a Labour Party pursuing a developmental policy associated with State issues of money is the tendency to restrict governmental activity to the sphere of the production or improvement of social utilities. There is always a danger of too great proportion of the funds of a Labour State being invested in the straightening of roads, in the establishment of new railway systems and similar works of national importance, the benefits from which are not immediately reflected in improved income. Yet the labour costs are liberated as immediate demand for consumption goods. On the contrary, the overdraft expenditure of business firms is generally utilised to facilitate the production of consumption goods. When

Opposing the Money Lenders

consumption goods are produced out of credit issues, the dangers of inflation are lessened.

A Government inhabiting a society halfway between Capitalism and Socialism, as in New Zealand, has to be very careful to see that the flow of consumption goods is maintained side by side with an increased production of social utilities. A Labour economy must all the time be interested in the quantity and quality of the goods and services which are the people's real income. A capitalist economy is not primarily concerned with the quantity and quality, but with the quantity of the profit, and too much expenditure on capital works might stimulate a demand for consumption goods and enable private enterprise to achieve a larger cash profit by an actual limitation of production, thereby creating inflation. In such a situation the community would have more social utilities, more conveniences, more educational institutions, more hospitals, better railways, better roads, better houses, but might conceivably have less of the multifarious requirements of the home. That situation has not occurred in New Zealand as a result of the policy pursued to date.

Cash values of consumption commodities produced have risen, but quantity production is also in the ascendant. The value of the guaranteed price to the State is that it is a price for a definite quality AND QUANTITY, and facilitates the production of consumption goods. How a State in this half-way house between Capitalism and Socialism can manage to apply, side by side with its Labour legislation, which restricts the hours of labour, the same stimulus to the production of boots and shoes and clothing, or whatever is required, that is has done in regard to butter, is not easy to see. In the half-way house of Socialism-Capitalism, the evils of both systems are likely to afflict us if we are not careful. Labour must stimulate the production of such quantities of goods as are necessary to New Zealand's welfare at an even higher standard. Capitalism cares only that the transaction yields a cash profit. To use a money machine only to create capital works and leave consumption goods to private finance is dangerous. Hence, at some stage Labour must give effect to the Prime Minister's intention of making credit available to secondary industry. Production that may not be profitable at the overdraft rates of the trading banks may be so socially desirable as to necessitate freeing it from the profit system so that quantities can flow to the extent required by the nation.

The Future: It will be seen that foundations have been laid for the establishment of a new financial system. Some say that: the Labour

John A. Lee

Government has advanced too rapidly in the field of money policy; some say with too great a timidity. Certain it is that while differences of opinion as to the degree of emphasis that has been given to this phase of Labour policy may vary in the Party, the difference in viewpoint between the most conservative member of the Party and the least conservative is only as to the speed of the advance, whereas the difference between the most conservative member of the Labour Party and the most progressive member of the opposing political party is an unbridgable gulf, the difference between the will to inhabit a profit system or the will to inhabit a system based on human requirements. The Labour Party is a democratic party and differences of opinion on the urgency of policy are from time to time discussed and decided by the vote of the majority. All want to move toward a common objective, but some would be content to crawl and then to walk. Some want to travel fast.

My own opinion is that as far as possible loans falling due in New Zealand should be taken over in their entirety by the Reserve Bank. There should be no re-borrowing from the private lender for State purposes except in regard to the Post Office Savings Bank, where interest ceases at an amount, or of superannuation funds. The private investor can have the field of private investment. Charges will be made that this would result in an inflation of prices. Well planned advances would cause goods to increase with money issues, and investment surpluses are not likely to be utilised by investors for the purpose of purchasing more food or more clothing or more of the necessities of life. The only inflation that would be likely to occur if investment surpluses became redundant would be an inflation in the price of gilt-edged securities and this would bring about a reduction in the rates of private lending and borrowing.

Who will finance housing at 2 per cent while the State pays 3 and a quarter per cent? There would be danger if the loans being paid off were likely to be utilised for purchasing the basic necessities of life, but people with investment surpluses already have the necessaries. It is true that in the event of our paying off our obligations as they fall due, we would increase the amount of deposits in the various trading banks and that some small portion of these deposits might seek to leave New Zealand to find investment elsewhere. It is unlikely that the average New Zealander would want London exchange under any circumstances, except for the purpose of buying imports or enjoying a holiday. The standard of living in New Zealand is so high that population is flowing in again, not away. The private banks cannot raid our London surplus while we have power to increase the amount of their deposits on time and demand liabilities, and there is for them no advantage in such a raid. They have the field of private lending after we have discontinued their power to be the nation's bondholders. Ample power is given today to the Reserve Bank to control the sale of exchanges and to impose checks where necessary.

The amounts of internal loan falling due are not large and would not dislocate New Zealand's economy or cause undue inflation. How else is a Labour State to prevent the eternal compounding of interest? We have no desire to expropriate or repudiate. All that we desire is to free the State from future liens on national development. The alternatives are confiscation, which Labour repudiates, or an agreement to condition Labour finance policy to Reformism within the private enterprise money system, that is, development of the nation out of loan moneys with interest compounding more rapidly than the service. If repayment caused investors to buy more of life's necessities than were being produced, there would be inflation. But no radical government was ever defeated by a mild rise in prices if purchasing power enabled production to be consumed. Actually, investors would buy private investments and mortgages and the rate of interest would fall. The inflation would be of New Zealand investments. Already in New Zealand, as a result of Reserve Bank underwriting at low rates, money is flowing to mortgage securities at 4 and a quarter per cent.

If Labour is only to run the Capitalist finance system, guaranteeing a permanent rate on all national development, the bailiff or the Hitler must arrive some day to collect. Issues for new production, whether of consumption of capital goods, if well planned, will not inflate, and if based on quantities, as are the guaranteed prices, will achieve stability. The repayment of internal loans would inflate only investments or exchange. If the loans were all falling due in a few years and not spread over decades, there would be dangers. But the alternatives, "A," expropriation, or "B," capitalism in perpetuity, to me seem packed with greater dangers.

Nothing has yet been done to make money available to the farmer or house builder at a lower rate of interest, but his indebtedness has been readjusted, his return enhanced and the 4 and one eighth per cent rate of the State Advances Department is not sacrosanct. Throughout all his political life, the Prime Minister has drawn attention to the necessity of using the State Bank to make funds available at a lower rate of interest to mortgagors. While nothing has yet been done, the Party is definitely pledged to move in that direction, and no doubt substantial steps toward that goal will be taken at some future date. Complete power has been won, some say it has been timidly exercised, some say it has been ruthlessly exercised. Extraordinary though it may seem, there is no great Press hostility to the principal of mortgages being reduced, because we are only interfering with a transaction, not with a system as when we interfere with interest. But, maybe, reduction of principal is a prelude to a cut in mortgage interest. After all, it requires a day or two for the new Government to achieve the maximum use of the new machine that has been created, and everything cannot be transformed in five minutes or in Labour's first Parliament. There is no doubt about the Labour Government's power. There is no reason to doubt what the tendency will be as Labour continues in office; else with all its magnificent expenditure on Public Works Labour only prepares a field day for the Capitalistic bailiff. This will not be!

With Banking, as with the Guaranteed Price, Labour prospers when the political enemy assails that for which Labour stands. The opposition advertise what the people want. And Democratic Governments are never defeated by rises in prices, provided the quantity of production is increasing and what is being produced is being distributed. Easing debt burdens is good democratic, as well as Labour policy.

This Debt Slavery : July, 1940, Budget Speech

A Harsh Orthodox Budget

MR. LEE (Grey Lynn).—Sir, this Budget is cast on more orthodox lines, although it is harsher to great wealth, than any Labour Budget yet introduced, and the criticisms from the Leader of the Opposition was an orthodox criticism. I heard the Prime Minister say that £400,000 was to be used for irrigation, and four millions for housing. All this money will bring goods into existence and add to our power to purchase. And yet, this Budget proposes to borrow under orthodox methods, even for the expenditure on housing. What is the need? The clay is in the hills, the timber is in the trees, we have the labour, we have the mills, the kilns, and I say that to the extent that we finance the building of a camp or of a house, or the pouring of water on to land, to add nine-fold, as the Minister of Public Works has stated, to the quantity, of goods produced, there is no reason why the people of New Zealand should be unnecessarily bled through taxation. The cost incurred will more than recoup itself in goods and services. Why not therefore issue instead of borrow?

Opposing the Money Lenders

Mr. Lee Moves Amendment

Therefore I propose to move, that the question be amended by omitting all the words after "that" with a view to inserting the following words in lieu thereof:-

"In the opinion of this House the Budget proposals are not acceptable without further revision and amendment, on the grounds:-

(1) They make no provision for the use of the public credit to increase New Zealand's internal production, (2) they increase the burden of internal debt, which will constitute a crushing liability on the people after the war, (3) the system of finance outlined in the Financial Statement is not calculated to enable the rehabilitation of the soldier after the war at the standard which is his right; and (4) they will reduce, without adding to the country's war effort, the consumption of food and other necessaries of life in thousands of New Zealand homes.'"

The Prime Minister broke issue with the Leader of the Opposition for suggesting that a measure of retrenchment was not likely to contribute to the Nation's war effort. I think that I and those who will support this motion are entitled to suggest that instead of the imposition of the wage tax on low incomes and the raising of funds by means of crushing taxation, we should make greater use of the public credit for the purpose of organising industry and producing fresh goods.

The Democratic Labour amendment will be seconded, and even if the mover and seconder fail to find another supporter they intend to divide the House, because although we may be unable to get anyone to vote in the Noes Lobby against the Budget, we at least think it wise to put on record the list of those voting for the wage cut and the orthodox financial system. I move that amendment, Mr. Speaker.

Orthodoxy Responsible For Unpreparedness

Now Sir, millions can die, nations can perish, the beast can straddle Europe, the black wings of bombing planes, I borrow a metaphor of Mussolini, can block the sun from the sky, but here in New Zealand orthodox finance must prevail, a people's control of the banking and finance machinery is not allowed to happen. The Budget is orthodox! More than any Budget produced yet by the Labour Government it shackles New Zealand to financial orthodoxy, even granting, as I will directly, that it contains some admirable features. The architect of the Budget learns nothing, loses none of his stubborn worship of financial orthodoxy, in fact I believe he is using this war to win a triumph for banking orthodoxy over the unorthodox members of the party. I am going to say that worship of financial orthodoxy is responsible for our lack of preparedness here in New Zealand more than anything else, our refusal to establish exchange control years ago, our refusal to interfere with orthodox money processes. Our refusal to force industrial production in New Zealand although we knew the production of consumption goods was absolutely essential if New Zealand was to know anything worthwhile in the form of a standard of living is due to worship of outmoded systems.

The Shrine Of St. Orthodox

This Budget has been patterned by those who worship at the shrine of St. Orthodox, who was born of stubbornness in Stupidity Street and cradled in cruelty. I believe that where the Budget demands sacrifice from wealth and accumulation it is a good Budget, because during a war wealth and accumulation must pay to safeguard wealth and accumulation. Men risk their lives. Wealth and accumulation must take a risk too. But where the Budget imposes unnecessary hardship upon those who consume goods that are in ample supply, the Budget imposes unnecessary hardship for the purpose of balancing itself on orthodox lines. There is much sacrifice in the Budget—the maximum. I do not think there is a great deal of leadership. I do not think the Budget is planned to create the maximum quantity of goods; it is planned to produce on orthodox lines the maximum quantity of money. Nor do I believe it is altogether a war Budget. I believe that to no small extent the Budget is patterned by the Labour Party's failure to impose certain necessary checks over the last few years.

Shortage Of Funds Due To Nash

On account of the shortage of sterling funds on the eve of the war, our industries were run down to the minimum of raw materials. What was that due to? I take as much responsibility as any member of the Labour Party, although I raise my voice in time. The shortage was due to the failure to conserve sterling funds at an early stage; due to the failure to force a greater proportion of our imports into capital investment so that we could produce consumption goods at a time like this. Due to Mr. Nash's short-sightedness, I say that financial orthodoxy is the cause of much of the shortage of goods with which we are confronted with today. Financial orthodoxy has failed the Labour Party all of the time.

Opposing the Money Lenders

Nash's Dilatoriness A Disaster

New Zealand also lost power to import goods as a result of Mr. Nash's dilatoriness in regard to the acquisition of foreign investments. Every other country at war, certainly every British country—took possession of foreign investments the moment war broke out when the price of the investments was high. We shilly shallied, and the value of external investments has fallen until investors rightly fear their investments may be sacrificed on a false market. If we had taken possession of those investments at the moment other nations were taking action, we would have secured greater foreign cash surpluses and we would have been enabled to import far greater quantities of raw materials, to buy more munitions, and the acquisition would have been fairer to the person dispossessed.

Too Late! Too Late!!

But always Mr. Nash is too late. Afraid to interfere with orthodox banking and financial systems in time, he is always dealing with effects. I look at the Reserve Bank return and I find that there is still in the vaults of the bank, gold valued at £2,800,000. Are we short of guns? Are we short of planes? Are we short of some piece of machinery to manufacture war equipment? £2,800,000 lies in the vaults of the Reserve Bank. Orthodox finance prevails. The soldier may yet be crucified on a cross of gold. What is that £2,800,000 doing in the bank? That gold should be mobilised to buy equipment, to bring in machinery we need, to buy raw materials we need, to get raw materials for New Zealand's consumption industries, to safeguard the Nation. But the gold lies in the vaults because of some absurd superstition we have that regardless of quantities of goods—regardless of the industry of the people, if that gold moves away the Nation falls. We are defending superstition instead of the Nation. But the nations of Europe have shipped their gold to the United States.

Goods Or Gold.

It is the capacity of British industry, the capacity of industry in the United States, which counts in war and in peace. In vaults in the United States there are hundreds of millions of gold. That gold is not going to defend democracy from the beast who straddles Europe, except that it liberates U.S.A. industry. I want to know what £2,800,000 is doing here in this emergency. Why is that gold not being sold to build New Zealand? Why is it not mobilized for our war effort? Is that £2,800,000 in the Reserve Bank to allow some orthodox director, some orthodox financial expert to pretend that £2,800,000 is, as it were, a strong point that is going to defend New Zealand democracy? We all know the £2,800,000 is not half as effective in the defence of New Zealand democracy as a machine-gun and a few sand-bags.

Wage Reduction Will Not Help War Effort

I do not believe the reduction in wages will help our war effort. Singularly enough, in the last six months of the war the workers of Britain have received an increase in wages. There have been increases in the agricultural industry, the cotton industry, a 10 per cent, in the steel industry, in Government engineering works, in dockyards, in soap and candle works. I feel that if there is going to be any reduction in the consumption of goods in New Zealand which is in part to be due to our war effort rationing should prevail rather than that there should be artificial curtailment of the consumption of imports by arbitrary reduction of everybody's wages. Those on the lower strata can scarcely afford to buy commodities that are plentiful now. They will not be able to afford to buy commodities that are plentiful after a reduction.

Five Years Of Nash's Cacanny

For five years there has been an advance on the industries front. For five years a good deal of procrastination too. For five years members of the Labour Party have wanted to interfere with orthodox trading processes to build up the nation. For five years we talked about the iron and steel industry, and tonight we are not even melting the pig-iron we need.

Are we to go on making investigation after investigation, securing report after report, and filling the pigeon-holes instead of getting things done because one individual is trying to control the destinies of the Nation? Because that individual is determined to worship at the shrine of Financial St. Orthodox, who was born of stubbornness in Stupidity Street, and cradled in cruelty? In regard to the rubber tyre industry we had investigation after investigation We talked of the sugar-beet industry, the paper industry. And what combinations we have seen opposed to new industry. The Press of the land wants cheap paper, while people who believe in orthodox trading processes are afraid to move. We have people who in the teeth of hostility set out to make cardboard. We are glad to have that cardboard today.

Opposing the Money Lenders

Industry Would Save More Life

In connection with public works we have heard that we build to save life. Yes, the new Paekakariki Road is a lovely if expensive road. The over-bridges on the road to Napier are very fine. They may have saved life, yes; but they did not save as much life as the same amount of concrete and steel poured into factories would have enabled us to nourish. We applaud the Minister of Public Works for building magnificent works because he had to find employment. But we should have been employing more people in factories. On the eve of last election, with exchange funds running low, we had woollen mills working half-time. Today we are advertising on the cinema-screens for operatives to return to the woollen industry. We lost opportunity to train operatives in 1938 because Mr. Nash would not interfere with orthodox money processes, with orthodox trading processes. Orthodoxy will not help us win the war. Financial orthodoxy will destroy the Labour Party.

Cheering Inefficient Pilots

The Conference of the Labour Party in 1939 cheered the failure to implement exchange control. I told that Conference, when it cheered, that I was reminded of passengers on the Empress of Ireland which sailed out of the St. Lawrence and ran into an iceberg on her way to Great Britain. We knew the funds were going out, funds required to build consumption industries to maintain our life. I cannot agree that the architect of delay, no, to alter my metaphor, the person who has repeatedly put the car into the ditch—is the only person to keep the car out of the ditch. St. Orthodox plunged us into difficulties and now we are told that St. Orthodox is the only fellow who can get us out of difficulties.

Ration Or Wage Cut

It is true that there will be a shortage of some imports due to war. The way to meet such a shortage is to ration rather than reduce the incomes of the lower sections of the community. We should not insist that only one stratum of the community should do with less imports. The shortage of consumption industries is due to lack of leadership and imagination, due to a determination not to handle any problem a day sooner than disaster. There was a ministerial determination to hang on to orthodoxy though the heavens fall. In the Budget the minister of finance sets his face against Reserve Bank borrowing.

John A. Lee

Ten Commandments — 200 Provisos

But if the Minister were to write ten commandments he would also write two hundred provisos. Thou shalt not borrow ! Provided that we may borrow in an orthodox way ! We find that in the Budget, We are told that we must pay war costs with taxation because if we borrowed we would inflate. And then we are told that nevertheless we may borrow in the private debt in perpetuity way. We have gold to the value of £2,800,000, and yet we require guns, explosives, industries.

Walter Over Hitler

The other night I had a political nightmare. Other people will have a nightmare soon. For one ghastly moment I visualised that Hitler landed on the shores of New Zealand, but that before he arrived every New Zealander except the Minister of Finance, was dead. We are pretty good fighters in New Zealand. The Minister was severely battered about because he can fight too, although he does bury his head in the sand. When the führer met him at the wharf he asked, "What have you got in New Zealand, Walter?" I heard a voice reply, "The only sound orthodox financial system an earth." With that we won the war because the Führer raised his hand, said "Heil," and dropped dead. (Laughter.) We are told that we must not borrow except we borrow in the orthodox way. We are told that to borrow through the Reserve Bank would be to inflate progressively. But we impose a 5 per cent, additional Sales Tax upon foodstuffs and upon wearing apparel, and we inflate the toilers cost of living. The Minister objects to inflating if inflation is unorthodox—if it does not pay its tribute to finance.

Disaster Followed Orthodoxy

The Minister talks of the disastrous effects which followed borrowing in the last war. The disastrous effects followed the borrowing methods the Minister proposes to use in this war. In Great Britain during the last war, when it was necessary to secure funds, Mr. Lloyd George started out by issuing Bradburys. Then the bankers brought pressure upon Mr. Lloyd George to allow the banks to issue the currency for war needs, but to issue the currency as debt and to charge the people of Britain 3, 4, 5 and finally, I believe, 6 per cent, in perpetuity. The war result was the same, but disaster followed, because the people had to pay interest on debt in perpetuity. Then St. Orthodox got us back to the gold standard and multiplied the weight of the debt of the war.

Debt Is Succeeded By Deflation

If we build debt during the war—and I say that we have to pay attention to these things now—to avoid the aftermath—we will have debt services absorbing our tax revenues, and there will be millions of unemployed demobilised soldiers reducing our markets at the same time. There will be a fall in prices with no expansion in producing power, and the world will be back to a crisis of poverty. Disaster must follow the borrowing methods the Minister now proposes. In New Zealand, during the last war, State securities were made the basis of an issue of currency. Thus, if a man subscribed £5 or £10 for a State bond, the bank advanced the £95 or the £90. The same will happen again if we utilise the compulsory loan provisions of the Budget. The people who will have the screw put on them will not have the money. They will be compelled to go to the bank to raise money. The money will be created as a private debt and will be a charge on the returning soldier and on New Zealand industry afterwards; whereas if issued as State Currency there would be no debt charge. Of course, the Minister argues that if we borrow the savings of the people we are not going to inflate, but if we create credit we will inflate.

The Four Hats Per Head Theory

What humbug. When a person has savings, he has something beyond his normal needs. The people who buy bonds have investment surpluses. Investors have enough butter, enough boots, enough hats. But the Minister reasons that if we issue instead of borrowing the people with money on deposit will withdraw the money and go along to the shops and buy three or four top hats, instead of one, that they will eat ten or eleven meals, instead of three, and that they will wear seven or eight pairs of socks at a time instead of one pair. We will keep to men's apparel. Everybody knows that will not happen, As a matter of fact, as fast as we issue notes, if we conscript the banking machinery—as we have conscripted the soldier — the money will return in the form of deposits.

An Intelligent Issue Creates Goods

Why should we borrow to build houses? We can issue to turn clay into bricks, to bring coal to brick kilns, to bring timber from the forest, as we have been doing. If we spend £100,000 manufacturing fertilizer in New Zealand, or adding to the value of raw material brought here to manufacture fertilizer, when that fertilizer is spread on the paddocks it will return goods far in excess of £100,000 in value. But though the heavens fall orthodoxy must prevail. Orthodoxy will not win this war. I am beginning to think that if the Minister of Finance goes on with his orthodox processes, he will succeed in placing New Zealand in such dire straits that finally, despite themselves, even the Opposition will become my converts, I admit that is a rather optimistic expectation.

Use Reserve Bank Credit

I believe that a large proportion of our war costs could be and should be met from Reserve Bank credit. When I say that, I mean that the Democratic Labour Party believes that too. The Official Labour Party used to believe it, and the majority of the Labour Party still believe it. I cannot agree with the reduction at the wage of the worker. I do not think it is necessary. I know how grave the war situation is, but even if the war situation were to swing still more against Britain— and we all trust, we know, we feel that Britain will win through—reduced wages will only add difficulty to our problems. Britain today commands the seas and Britain is going to prevent the primary-producing countries of the world sending produce to France, Belgium, Holland, Norway, Sweden and all the other countries that were substantial consumers of that primary produce. If much of Britain's mercantile marine is destroyed it will reduce our capacity to export.

Britain Needs Tonnage, Not Extra Food

Given tonnage Britain will have difficulty in consuming all of the foodstuffs that are available. There is no need to cut incomes of workers in New Zealand when we know that a reduction will curtail the consumption of foodstuffs of which we have adequate supplies in New Zealand.

Money Instrument Of Production

I read in the Budget that money is only worth what can be purchased with it. But money is worth more than what can be purchased with it.

Money is an instrument which can bring into being goods to be purchased. Where there are idle men and machines and where there is idle material, where there is potential production, money can be used to facilitate production. Yet nowhere in the Budget do we feel that the finance is to be used to add to wealth, to build up welfare. The monetary mechanism is only being used for the purpose of squeezing the last ounce out of existing industry. To win the war we need to look further than the goods now in existence. Britain could not win with the war materials that she had after her defeat in Flanders. She will win with the tanks, the guns, the high explosives and the planes that are being and will be brought into existence; with the food that will be shipped to Britain, the food that will be produced during the war. We must get it out of our minds that money can only purchase existing goods. Money, plus intelligent organization, can organise production and can make potential production into actual goods.

Wanted Farmer Finance

We call upon the farmer to produce more goods. What are we doing to assist him in the production of goods? Despite the fact that we will have difficulty in getting rid of our surpluses, as the Prime Minister said, we have got to face up to the necessity for producing more goods, to the necessity of building up our population in New Zealand and building up a more balanced economy in New Zealand. We have to remember that the time is going to come when the wild beast of Europe will be halted, when much in the way of food and goods will be needed, and for humanitarian reasons as well as for patriotic reasons, it is necessary that we should build up our production of primary produce at this moment even if we cannot see a market. But what are we doing to make cheap credit available to the farmer so that he can develop his industry? We give him men and we subsidise fertilizers. But when it comes to cheap credit the State Advances Department is governed, not by the will of the people who want an advance, but by the policy determined by this House, by the funds made available. To what extent are we willing to finance the farmer to extend production so that he can increase his output of primary products without increasing his debt in perpetuity?

Salvation Or Suicide

Let us glance at the war costs. We are going to spend about £20,000,000 a year overseas, and we are going to borrow that money. Now I am going to say this at the risk of being misunderstood, that borrowing money in Britain to buy Britain's output of war materials, does not add anything to the sum total of the Empire's war effort. We can give what we have—our men and the materials we produce—but as Britain's industries produce armaments and as Britain buys armaments from the United States with liquidated investments or with sales of gold,

John A. Lee

I do not see why we should borrow in Britain to buy the proceeds of such liquidated investments. It is fairly obvious that if we now borrow £20,000,000 a year, £30,000,000 or £40,000,000—if the war flares to a greater degree of violence—and if we build up external debts of £300,000,000 to £400,000,000 we will not be helping the Empire's war effort, but only placing New Zealand into an intolerable bondage in future. It is not unpatriotic to discuss and face up to this question.

Crazy Finance

We can only borrow abroad to buy the munitions of some other part of the Empire if we get a long-term guarantee for our produce at a high price. If we were borrowing to bring into the Empire pool something that was not there we would be justified, I think that we should say to Britain, and there is nothing unpatriotic about it, that this is a time for pooling war resources. Let us enter into a long-term agreement to contribute a certain amount of goods, let us enter into an agreement to contribute everything in the nature of manpower that we can without weakening the defence of New Zealand. But again I want to say that merely borrowing to buy the output of British industry or to buy munitions produced by the United States and purchased by Britain with liquidated British investments and the sale of gold, does not add one fraction to Great Britain's war effort, nor to the British Empire's war effort, but it does permanently place this country in a position of bondage after the war is over to the overseas financiers.

Land For Heroes

And after all we do want a world fit for heroes to live in. We do want men to return to this country after grappling with the Beast to enjoy a decent standard of living. The Budget says:— "To the extent that this borrowing arrangement is utilized we will be piling up deadweight overseas debt. That will be a heavy burden on us for many years after the war, when our ability to pay may be less than it is now." So we face a lessened ability to pay, a burden of debt multiplied by two. That is not salvation, it is suicide. I would not make the point if borrowing added one ounce, one bullet, to the Empire's war effort, but actually we are borrowing to take up munitions produced by other portions of the Empire. We can contribute what we have, but it is not fair to engage in a commitment that will leave our industries, and our soldiers who fight, crippled for the next few decades.

Opposing the Money Lenders

Defence, And New Zealand Problem

I think the events of the last few weeks have compelled us to realise that we have to change our attitude to defence too. The defence of Empire for New Zealand becomes the defence of Auckland, Wellington, Christchurch and Dunedin.

Empire patriotism for the New Zealand House of Parliament begins right here—begins in New Zealand. We have won a lot of wars. We have got to win the peace as well. We have got to erect a decent New Zealand here when the beast is toppled from supremacy in Europe.

Motherhood Endowment For Every Child

We note with pleasure the portion of the Budget which promises to take another child into the motherhood endowment scheme. I live for the day when the Labour Government, in the light of the policy placed before the people at the last election, will set out to improve motherhood endowment—to make the endowment of motherhood commence with the first child. This House should give the mother a reward for the contribution she is making, not only to New Zealand's industries but actually to New Zealand's defence. We have got to think in terms of defence a long way ahead, because it might just happen that after we temporarily solve the problem in Europe other problems are likely to occur round about the Pacific. Anything we can do to ease the burden of the mother should be done. We should start, I believe, with the first child, and regardless of the family income. What a socialist Government should recognise is that the mother contributes a service to the State when she brings into existence one child and cares for that child, and we should make the mother adequate allowance. A married man with two children under the Budget scheme will not only pay his increased 5 per cent, but I think he will pay about £72 on an income of £500. A single man on £500 will pay £97. Nobody can convince me that the married man keeps a wife and two children for the sum of £25. There is no equality of sacrifice there—none whatsoever.

May Impose Hardship

A National Security Tax of 4 to 5 shillings a week, says the Budget, may impose some degree of hardship. There will be a 5 per cent Sales Tax on children's boots and shoes, on their little pullovers, and all the other things they wear? Listen to the words. "May impose some degree of hardship." What has happened to the author of the Budget? Once upon a time he would have said unmistakably, will impose hardship. The banking Pharaohs' have hardened his heart. I am at a loss to understand the language, "May impose some degree of hardship." I think, frankly, it would be better to dent the orthodox financial system a little and exempt the toiler on this low standard of income.

We are going to have primary produce redundant in New Zealand. There is no reason at all why the food standard of families should be reduced in any way whatsoever. Costs will rise because of the increased cost of imports. Local costs because of the 5 per cent, sales tax.

Where there are few imports, let us ration, let us give everybody a fair share, but where there is an abundant supply of local commodities why reduce wages for the purpose of getting a financially balanced Budget if we are going to curtail the consumption of goods that are abundant? That is what we are doing.

Of course, I know that the wages tax is imposed upon the rich and the poor. I think it was Anatole France who once said—I forget the exact words— "The law in its majesty forbade both the rich and the poor the right to beg, the right to sleep under bridges, the right to starve to death" I forget the exact words; it is a long time since I used the quotation.

State Advances For Companies

When we come to company taxation I am reminded again of a magnificent part of the Labour Party's programme, "Advances to build up industries." The advances are not being made, or they are being made after inquiry, after investigation on investigation, report after report. Advances should be made, and I suggest that if goods are the problem where we are taxing a company that can produce an additional quantity of consumer goods needed at the moment, we would be wise if we had same swift means of allowing that Company to re-absorb the whole of its taxes in permanent industrial expansion. We could make the tax a State advance to the industry a State investment in the industry. We used to talk that way before we started to worship at the shrine of St, Orthodox.

War Does Not Purge

I am interested in the Budget's philosophy. The Budget says:— "The cause of truth and justice will ultimately prevail and ... the democratic

Opposing the Money Lenders

institutions of the world will survive the purging fire of the forces of Oppression." Believe me, there are no purging fires about war. War is not good; it does not purge, it destroys. It is a foul, hideous beast, and we only go to war because Fascism is foul; not because war is noble, but because we have to choose between war and the hideous beast of Fascism which is fouler still. Do not talk about the purging fires of war. Hitler and war, here they are:

> "Lastly came anarchy; He rode
> On a white horse splashed with blood,
> On his brow this mark I saw I am God and King and Law."

There are no purging fires about that. I recommend the Minister to read Sassoon's poem, "They" I only quote one verse: -

> "The Bishop tells us, when the boys come back
> They will not be the same
> For they have fought in a just cause
> They lead the last attack on anti-Christ."

I will not quote the rest. War is foul. It will leave its mark on everybody who takes part in it. But Fascism is fouler, and that is the only reason why everybody must accept this challenge. Fascism is literally a nation at war all of the time, even in a state of peace, the militarised state in perpetuity. And in the Budget I note with interest the quotation from the Saint, and a good quotation:-

> "To give and not to count the cost,
> To fight and not to heed the wounds,
> To toil and not to seek for rest,
> To labour and not ask for any reward."

But the Saint was stating what he himself should do and was appealing to others to make a sacrifice. We have to appreciate that the Budget, to no small extent, is a vicarious atonement. It is a different proposition altogether. We are not entitled to put the taxpayer on the cross and say to him :— "To give and not to count the cost"; we are not entitled to put a nail into the soldier and say :— 'To fight and not to heed the wounds". That quotation is personal. When we are preparing a Budget that puts the family on the cross, and that reduces the foodstuffs on the table, we should take count of every penny of the cost and discover whether there are any alternative means of avoiding the wage cuts that will bring hardship to the humblest homes. While the soldier must go forward when the challenge arises, risking everything and not heeding the wounds, we must remember that when we send him forward we have to count every drop of blood. There must be no unnecessary sacrifice. We must see to it that we achieve victory with the least possible damage to those who, in their generosity and patriotism, have entrusted their young manhood to our care. "To toil and not to seek for rest, to labour and not to ask for any reward."— I hope that all who labour in this war will ask finally for a better New Zealand, and for a world at peace. The Saint was labouring for heaven; we are not so much concerned about the hereafter of the people as members of this House, but we are concerned about the people's present.

No Unnecessary Sacrifice

We must be careful we do not inflict unnecessary punishment, that we do not risk lives unnecessarily, that we do not shed a drop of blood we can avoid shedding. We have to see to it that as we sacrifice others through our legislation we do our best to see that they achieve the reward of a New Zealand fit for heroes to live and a New Zealand that will play a Great Nation's part in the world of peace that is to be. If the Labour Party's financial programme were given effect to now, as I would give effect to it, as the Democratic Labour Party would give effect to it, and as the seconder of this motion would give effect to it, I believe that we would ease the burden of thousands of our people in New Zealand without in any way destroying our war effort. Indeed by being more generous and by producing a Budget which aimed at creating the maximum amount of goods rather than at squeezing the maximum of money from the people, we could produce in New Zealand that warring spirit that would make our people still more willing to go forward to win the battle that lies in front of us.

MR. ATMORE (Nelson).—Mr. Speaker, I second the amendment.

The House divided on the question, "That the words proposed to be omitted stand part of the question."

AYES, 63. NOES, 2. Atmore. Lee. Majority for, 61. Amendment negatived.

Opposing the Money Lenders

A Letter which Every New Zealander should Read

To All Members Of
The Parliamentary Labour Party

I am alarmed at the present evidence of indecision, vacillation and drift which is apparent within the Party. I am concerned for the future welfare of the Labour Party, not for its right to exist as an entity returning Members to Parliament as caretakers of a capitalist system, but for its right to exist as a driving force, effecting fundamental changes in the "boom and bust" capitalist system. I am fearful that at any moment a statement may be made that we are going to increase the internal interest rate, which to me, would be a betrayal of a major order, especially after emerging victoriously from an election in which the people defeated Money Power.

As I write, exchange control has occurred, but to every intelligent person it must be obvious that control arrives two years in arrears, after finance has looted the London Cash Box. To everyone it must be obvious that exchange control has arrived now not as a positive virtue for the purpose of safeguarding the future of the working class party in this country by preventing gangster finance from raiding our external exchanges, but that it has at long last been implemented because the raid has rendered the sterling cash box empty, and exchange control is the only alternative to default.

Since I think that Mr. Nash, in his approach towards financial policy suited to Labour's ideals, is always likely to be two or three years in arrears, it is well at this stage to outline how the problem of control of our exchanges as a portion of our financial policy appealed to other members of the Party who desired to install a new financial policy and at the same time take steps to prevent the Labour movement from being wrecked by financial gangsters. Only by studying Mr Nash's dilatoriness may we save ourselves from future dangerous delay. In *Labour Has a Plan,*" written by myself for the Party in November-December, 1934, the following appeared: —

"It seems as if there are limits to Britain's power to absorb our primary commodities, or at least until there is a great policy of social spending in Britain. Inevitably this means that the external surplus available for imports will not be nearly sufficient to supply our New Zealand needs in manufactures under a policy of intelligent consumption.

John A. Lee

In the past, when the demand for importers' credit exceeded the supply, the banker became our fiscal dictator. He issued credit to the importer with an eye on the transaction's financial profit. Labour says that when the demand for importers' credit exceeds the supply the people and not a group of bankers should determine how the credit is to be allotted. With a rising internal standard of living it will be increasingly found that our export surplus will have to be utilised for the purchase of those goods we cannot economically make. Certainly, if we lifted our internal income to the pre-slump level there would be a demand for imports far in excess of our annual supply of external credit, a demand which was met in the past, year after year, out of borrowed funds...."

I do not claim this paragraph as evidence of unusual discernment. It was just evidence of the commonsense in regard to finance which seems to afflict nearly every member of the Party except the Minister of Finance, and which seems to cause Caucus members to be excluded from control of finance policy. It was apparent that we could not leave high local incomes without action to ensure that these incomes were used;

1. To sustain local industry to its maximum productivity.

2. To enable New Zealand to consume its sterling surplus after we had ear-marked sufficient exchange for debt services.

To quote again from "Labour has a plan":—

"We shall want every penny of external credit to buy what we cannot make or cannot grow."

Early in 1937 I wrote a propaganda pamphlet, *"Money Power for the People,"* in which I expressed on Page 12, the following:—

"In terms of the original Act, the Reserve Bank was given complete control over the ownership of sterling exchange (London funds) subject to the necessity of making exchange available, under certain conditions, on demand .... This power is of vital importance as it arms the Government with power to control those internal movements of gangster finance capital that can occur in times of political emergency and that can do grave harm to a country's industries, that can raid a country's external credit."

Opposing the Money Lenders

And on Page 13, I illustrated another sort of power which could have been used to prevent foreign controlled banks, i.e., Australian, from raiding our funds:—

"Under Section 45 of the principal Act of 1933 provision was made for the trading banks to lodge balances with the Reserve Bank to the extent of 3 per cent, of their time liabilities and 7 per cent, of their demand liabilities. Clause 2 of the Amending Act gave the Minister of Finance power to cause, by notice published in the Gazette, the Governor of the Bank to vary upward or downward the balance required to be maintained by any bank. This power enables the Minister of Finance to check inflation by causing trading banks to deposit a greater proportion of their time and demand liabilities, and this power also arms the Minister with authority which effectively enables him to resist any efforts on the part of trading banks to raid London Funds by compelling the Trading Banks to maintain such New Zealand balances as the Minister thinks fit"

On Pages 15 and 16 of the same pamphlet I said,—

"In the terms of the Act, the Reserve Bank of New Zealand owns all London exchange and under certain circumstances may absolutely refuse such London exchange and under certain circumstances may absolutely refuse such London exchange to anyone. This power to refuse London funds is a necessary power and allows an opportunity for the Bank to be used at a later date for the purpose of a planned economy in New Zealand. .... While at the present moment the Bank is selling exchange freely in the manner of all capitalistic banking institutions, a day may arrive when Government will seek to assist New Zealand industry and maybe assist the industry of Great Britain or any country with which New Zealand has an exchange balance, through a more careful scrutiny of the use to which external funds are put. At the present moment the power to refuse exchange is not being utilised and there appears to be no immediate likelihood of its use, short of an attempt by gangster finance to raid London funds. .... On March 30th, 1936, the sterling exchange available in London to the Government amounted to £24,830,101,— a very handsome inheritance for a Labour Government desiring to carry through a policy calculated to bring New Zealand into conflict with international banking hostility. About £3,000,000 worth of New Zealand stock has been redeemed in Great Britain, thereby reducing the external public debt and saving a very large amount of interest to the Public Accounts. Notwithstanding this redemption, on April 19th, 1937, the London exchange funds amounted to £19,622,337 0s. 19d, — a very fine position for a Labour Government threatened with such alarmist attacks as have occurred during the past few days in the *"Evening News"* in London, attacks which render it the more necessary to keep London funds high to safeguard New Zealand against privately-controlled gangster capital."

I could not then say that exchange should be controlled or that we intended to control exchange. To make such a suggestion in a pamphlet would have created difficulties, but at that moment and at nearly every meeting of the Caucus where finance was discussed, I was urging that some action should be taken to build up New Zealand by the control of sterling exchange and to ear-mark such sums as would be needed overseas for us to fight our political enemies. But this action was not due to any omniscience on my part. It merely reflected the commonsense of the Caucus generally. I only record my opinion because I have written testimony of my attitude. The only reason for not moving a resolution to control exchange was that we secured a definite assurance that exchange would be controlled, and, accepting this, we agreed it would not be wise to carry such a resolution lest the information leak out. True, there were some opposed to exchange control although not one of those could suggest any alternative.

My pamphlet written in 1937 and probably by some members of the Party thought to be too aggressive, because it reiterated the policy upon which we won our mandate in 1935, was only representative of Caucus. The Party pushed for exchange control and for local industrial development until it became dangerous to push any further for those things on account of each finance movement in Caucus being met with irritation, by threats of resignation, and by suggestions that those who wanted to do the right thing to give effect to our principles were being disloyal to the Party.

Dr. McMillan, in his able memorandum, dated 29th November, 1937, set out the position to the Party, a position apparent to everyone except those who control financial policy. Some of the Doctor's points are worth repeating:—

Said the Doctor:

"Depletion of overseas funds can be dealt with in three ways -

1. Borrowing in Great Britain.

Opposing the Money Lenders

This is one of the expedients which has been adopted in the past and it obviously necessitates a domestic policy which will keep the confidence of, and meet the wishes of, the overseas moneylender, e.g., this gentleman is obviously opposed to our taking over the Bank of New Zealand. He would require, as the price of his confidence wages and pension cuts when overseas prices fall, and if prices fall before its introduction, the serious curtailment of coming social legislation. Though all members of the Government are opposed to the policy of overseas borrowing and subservience to overseas money lenders, unless we are very careful we will be manoeuvred into taking that step and all its unfortunate and tragic sequelae. Unless we make preparation in advance, unless we deal with causes instead of results, every retrograde step will be the logical one to take.

2. By contracting credit in New Zealand to produce a depression here to lower the standard of living of the people, and reduce the demand for imports, thereby relieving the strain on our overseas funds.

(This has already been done. John A. Lee) Credit has not been restricted in the immediate past, but if internal prices fall and margins run off, Banks which wish to avoid bankruptcy will be obliged to call in loans.....

3. By rationing exchange and developing secondary industries.

"I submit, Sir (said the Doctor), "that to travel any road but this one must cause our people acute distress and lead to our failure. This third alternative enables the Government to conserve the country's overseas funds, but hand in hand with a rationed exchange must go a vigorous development of secondary industries."

As I have said, Caucus was given to understand that exchange control was to come and that resolutions would not be wise, and members accepted that statement. And so the drift continued up until the eve of the election, at which moment, of course, remedial action was impossible. Nothing had been done while the financial gangsters were raiding our exchanges, and only now, in arrear, to prevent a positive default, is anything being done.

And so today we are dealing with effects because we refused to deal with causes; indeed, those who wanted to deal with causes were treated as children and disloyalists. Implemented two years ago, exchange control could have been introduced with a tight rein. Now, it will have to be introduced with a savage curbed bit. The political goodwill associated with doing things willingly and in time was sacrificed through vacillation and drift. The control which would have safeguarded a sterling nest-egg against our London refunding obligation, enabling us to meet banking hostility, becomes a control to prevent a default, and with the cupboard so bare that Labour may be driven to pay the British money-lender's price for re-funding the £17,000,000 loan. And yet we pretend that we have been faithful trustees of the Labour Movement with the interests of the voters at heart. And to the extent that we are forced to too hastily accumulate London funds, exchange control will have a political harshness completely unnecessary had we acted in time. Our incursion into exchange control will be in political effect like the result of our Guaranteed Price Advisory Committee, which completely wrecked the guaranteed price as a political asset at the last General Election, probably costing us all the butter seats, which was to be expected when Labour appointed a Committee of such arch-Tories as Sir F.V. Fraser, Messrs G.A. Duncan, H.M. Casselberg, N.H. Moss, C.P. Agar, A.H. Tocker, and L.A. Marshall to interpret our policy, instead of trusting the commonsense and goodwill of its own members assembled in Caucus. For we must not, only do the right thing but the right thing the political way.

Labour Finance Policy

It is well to appreciate that the Conference of the New Zealand Labour Party in April, 1933, adopted a financial policy which was re-affirmed in April, 1934, and upon which the Party fought the election of 1935. The policy read:

> "Immediate control by the State of the entire banking system. The State to be the sole authority for the issue of credit and currency. Provision of credit and currency to ensure production and distribution of the commodities which are required and which can be economically produced in the Dominion, with guaranteed prices, wages and salaries."

It is true that Mr. Nash has told Caucus that about twenty years are necessary to give effect to this Policy, but most of us believe that the word "immediate" meant what it said and that immediate control is practicable, is essential.

It is worthwhile to have a look at the banking progress to date.

More Debt

We took over the Reserve Bank to free Labour development from capitalist debt, but showed our lack of faith in Labour's policy by paying £6 5s. for a £5 share and by paying with 4 per cent, debentures instead of buying out the shares with Reserve Bank currency, a far more generous treatment in the first session than Mr. Nash proposed for the old-age pensioner.

We did the same thing, of course, with the Mortgage Corporation, paying a premium of $^1/3$ on each 10s share or alternatively issuing 4 per cent stock for share and premium. We should have retired both forms of share with Reserve Bank currency.

The first important financial transaction conducted by the Reserve Bank was the re-funding of our loan. It will be remembered that we agreed to borrow new money at 3¼ per cent, and to refund at 3¼ per cent. It is interesting to contrast this action with the statements of the Prime Minister, which were characteristic of the statements of nearly everyone in the party. Certainly I found myself in 100 per cent alignment with those statements. Speaking in Dunedin prior to the date of the election in 1935, the Prime Minister said:

> "The three alternatives are taxation, borrowing or intelligent use of credit. The Parliamentary and banking machine will be set in action to use credit."

Speaking in Auckland he said:

> "The net interest payments on the public debt for twenty years ending 1934 amounted to £141,132,472. Was it to be a debt in perpetuity, like a snowball gathering as it went along? If the War Cabinet had dealt with public credit as it should have done, there would be no War Debt to-day."

Which statement shows that Mr. Savage has no love for the debt system. Speaking to the "Dominion" following the election, the Prime Minister said:

> "Borrowing from the public for the purpose of spending could not be supported. The State would have to accept full responsibility for finance."

John A. Lee

The Party's Manifesto had said:

> "A planned economy will be of little use if the Government has not the proper power to carry its plans into effect. Such power will require the control of credit which, if it remains in private hands, can be used to thwart the will of the Government."

I was then of the opinion and am still that we should have used the powers of the Reserve Bank to wipe out most of the indebtedness although exchange control would have been necessary to prevent the raiding of sterling exchanges. We should have at least compelled the refunding at a much lower interest rate. When this was suggested in Caucus, we had all the capitalist arguments advanced against the proposal by Mr. Nash. Such an action, he said, would mean inflation; as if people with sufficient incomes and investment surpluses eat twice as much goods and buy twice as much clothing when they cannot buy bonds at a high rate. Actually, the rate of borrowing on account of our forcing money into circulation would have declined immensely. Investment surpluses are spent on the production of capitalist goods, not consumables, hence indeed the whole basis of the socialist attack on capitalism i.e. too much capital goods, too little consumption, hence the undistributed surplus loading to unemployment crises. But Mr. Nash sets aside the whole nature of the capitalist crisis and pretends that investment surpluses will become consumer income if socialism tries to find its way out of the debt system. If we are always to be daunted by the inflation bogey, debt is with us forever.

To me, refunding the whole loan at the 3¼ per cent rate of interest inherited from the Coalition Government was a complete betrayal of our promises to the people. But worse was to come. After agreeing to refund at 3½ per cent, and on the eve of Mr Nash's departure for London, Caucus was called hastily together and without previous warning Mr. Nash moved a resolution that 3½ per cent be the rate for our refunding obligations. I had the honour, with others, to oppose that resolution verbally and by vote, although I had just received my appointment as Under-Secretary in Charge of Housing. Fifty per cent, of the Caucus voted against the ¼ per cent increase. We were told at that Caucus that the alteration was necessary to create a good atmosphere for Mr. Nash in London, that is, that Labour has to be good. We may be told the same again directly in regard to our £17,000,000 London loan, the shilly-shallying and drifting having allowed the New Zealand people to be put into a position where their interests have been worsened to the advantage of raiding financial gangsters.

Opposing the Money Lenders

It was only in arrear of the decision to increase the refunding rate to 3½ per cent, that the real inwardness of the increase was understood. Only after Mr. Nash's departure did the news start to filter through that the Reserve Bank Board, then composed of anti-Labour Directors, were whooping with joy for they had carried a resolution that 3½ per cent, instead of 3¼ per cent, be the underwriting rate for our loan. This decision of the Reserve Bank Board was not communicated to Caucus. It is doubtful if it were communicated to all members of Cabinet, although it must have been communicated to some members of Cabinet. Thus, at the first challenge of conservative finance Labour retreated allegedly to make an easier London atmosphere for Mr. Nash, although what London gave us for our surrender I have yet to ascertain.

With the low rate of interest, say 2½ per cent, and exchange control to prevent the raiding of sterling, we would have forced funds into the development of New Zealand industries. It is idle to pretend that to make an issue to pay our internal stocks is to cause the prices of consumables to rise. The moneys that are waiting to be lent are the investment surpluses of people who already have all the requirements of a decent standard of existence and are moneys liberated against the production of capital goods or for the purpose of gilt-edged securities, and not moneys liberated for articles of consumption. Those members of Caucus who voted for 3¼ per cent, as against 3½ per cent, (the rate dictated by the reactionary Reserve Bank Board) were not made any more popular thereby. Indeed, as men fight to give effect to the financial pledges of the Party to the people, they become more unpopular among those who control the financial policy of the Labour Party.

Local Body Loans

All members of Caucus can remember the conflict which occurred in regard to the provision of loans for local bodies. We had pledged ourselves to the people to make funds available from a State Credit institution for Local Body development. Time and time and time again this matter was raised in Caucus, and with increasing irritation from high places toward those who raised it. Mr. Nash wrote letters to local bodies suggesting the hypothecation of local body debentures to private banking interests on an overdraft basis when they wrote seeking loan funds for necessary works. Meanwhile, local bodies were finding subsidised work for unemployed men out of state funds because they could not get loan moneys for necessary works.

Even to-day, the term set for loans to local bodies by the State Advances Corporation is far too short. In this morning's paper ("Dominion", 7th December, 1938) I find the Masterton County Council stating that it can only get £1,500 of a £11,500 loan it requires for bridge repairs and replacements for a period of 10 years on a 20 years amortization table, the balance at the end of the tenth year becoming payable in one sum. The Council, faced with the necessity of renewing at the end of ten years, will probably go on arguing the point about doing the job instead of getting on with the necessary work. The State Advances exchequer is probably empty because of failure to implement the finance policy upon which the Labour Government pledged itself to the people of New Zealand.

Personally, I never saw one of Mr. Nash's letters to local bodies to hypothecate their scrip to the private banking interests reproduced in the Press without a feeling of shame at this betrayal of the policy we had pledged ourselves to, for Mr. Nash was certainly not giving effect to Labour's election policy. Again the members of the Party who repeatedly brought up in Caucus the necessity of making loans to local bodies found themselves being stigmatised as wreckers, assassins, etc. Today, local bodies are getting a portion of their funds for terms altogether too short, after they have unsuccessfully hawked their securities to every private financing institution.

I still believe that the Party pledged itself that funds necessary to build New Zealand nationally or by any local body should be found by the people for the people from the people's banking service, and because some of us thought that the letters asking local bodies to hypothecate their securities to private banks were shameful betrayals of Party policy, we were marked down as malingerers.

Restriction Of Loans

To-day, we approach another crisis. Because through shilly-shallying and lack of policy and drift we deal with results and not with causes, and because we are introducing exchange control after the London Cash Box is virtually empty, i.e., because the alternative is default and not because of the will to conserve funds to protect New Zealand from paying a too high rate of interest, we have brought down upon ourselves other problems. Failure to prevent the transfer of deposits has caused such a withdrawal of local deposits for the purpose of raiding our exchanges, that the basis of trading bank advances has been undermined and the Bank of New Zealand is refusing overdrafts

Opposing the Money Lenders

to industry and is calling up overdrafts at a moment at which we are about to ask New Zealand industry to expand as never before. Our banking and finance policy was as follows,—again let me repeat the terminology of Conference:

"Immediate control by the State of the entire banking system. The State to be the sole authority for the issue of credit and currency. Provision of credit and currency to ensure production and distribution of the commodities which are required and which can be economically produced in the Dominion, with guaranteed prices, wages and salaries."

With a magnificent majority we controlled the Reserve Bank very largely on orthodox lines. Nothing was done to make credit available to industry by taking over a trading bank. An Act was passed authorising the State Advances Corporation to supply funds for new industry in conformity with our policy, but to date this Act is pure showmanship. Nothing was done to make the State the sole authority for the issue of credit and currency which would have at least necessitated ownership and control of the Bank of New Zealand. Resolutions were moved in Caucus and were withdrawn on the assurance of the Prime Minister that a Bill would be prepared during the first recess. Next time the matter was raised, the taking over of the Bank was opposed by Mr. Nash for a variety of reasons. "It would cost too much." "We did not have men to administer the legislation." "The State would have to determine who should have overdrafts." Of course, the fact that until the State does determine for what purpose funds shall be available we are perpetuating a system we are pledged to destroy, did not bother Mr. Nash. And, of course, one of the great difficulties at the moment confronting the Party is the god-like attitude of the Minister of Finance who assumes that he is the only one capable of affecting any transformation, although in truth he is the Party's most refractory instrument. When the Party persisted with a resolution to take over the Bank, we had the Prime Minister telling us-.

(1) We could have his resignation;

(2) That if we carried the resolution he would not agree to do the job anyhow.

I honestly believe the Prime Minister was with the resolution but felt that he had to stick to his Minister.

John A. Lee

Again we had the spectacle of the men fighting for our policy being described as wreckers, malingerers, assassins, etc. After telling us he would not heed Caucus's vote, many members left the Caucus and then the vote was actually taken at 1.15 p.m., after many who believed in taking over the Bank had left Caucus because they were not prepared to precipitate a personal crisis. Even then, the vote was a dead-heat, members, such as Mr. Gordon Hullquist, who was in favour of the immediate taking over of the Bank, not wanting to force a breach with the Prime Minister, and regretfully voting against his convictions and Labour's policy.

Calling Up Of Overdrafts

And now today we are caught again dealing with effects because we refused to alter causes. The unchecked transfer of funds to capitalism to London has undermined the present legal basis for bank advances. We are about to ask New Zealand industry to expand, and while we are calling for expansion scores of solvent businesses are having the screw put upon them and are being asked to reduce their overdrafts. Where this restriction applies to imports, it should have been applied long since. Where it applies to local woollen mills, etc., which are being asked to expand, it is wicked and does not conform to Labour's principles. Carried far enough, it will cause a rise in unemployment of the crisis order, and maybe a spectacular bankruptcy or two.

What are we to do, someone will say, if the Bank of New Zealand has not the legal right to make advances and sustain production or if the Reserve Bank has not the authority to buy Government securities from the Bank of New Zealand to provide the necessary funds? We are so wedded to orthodox finance and not to local prosperity or Labour policy that we look with horror upon each increase in Reserve Bank advances to the State. When the sterling raid is checked and while prices are not rising dangerously, we should look with favour upon each increase for it will represent income circulated by Labour in addition to what could be circulated under the orthodox process, and if we show a firm front, we shall soon borrow on our own terms. What, we are to do to prevent the present wholesale calling up of overdrafts which is likely to restrict consumption and production? First of all, to be heartily ashamed of the way the vital plank in our programme was allowed to be defeated and delayed by the Minister of Finance after the people had given Labour a tremendous majority in Parliament and after that majority had wanted to give effect to their pledges. If the State has not power to allow the Bank of New Zealand to make

Opposing the Money Lenders

greater advances, let the Reserve Bank advance to the Bank of New Zealand against State securities held by the Bank. And, for Heaven's sake, if legislation is required, let Parliament meet at once to pass the legislation. We have been dragged heels first into exchange control; cannot we handle this situation in advance instead of bungling along in our characteristic style? While we are in the shadow of the greatest crisis and the greatest opportunity ever given to a Labour Government, every member of the Party should be in Wellington dealing with bold principles, but we head for Niagara with the Party locked out.

Increase In The Bank Rate

A published decision of the Reserve Bank has recently laid it down that the Reserve Bank believes that 4 per cent, should be the rate for short-term loans. A cable from the London "Sunday Times" suggests that the rate for local Treasury Bills has been increased to 4 per cent. This statement has been published in the Local Press and appears to be common property but has been neither affirmed or denied. I am unable to say whether the increase has been made good or not, but if the rate for Treasury Bills has been increased to 1 per cent, and if we allow that increase to be maintained we again, after Inning emerged from a General Election with an overwhelming majority, agree to betray our policy and the people of New Zealand. If we accept the so-called market rate of money conversion, control of credit and currency on behalf of the people is dead.

I know, as one of the Committee of Conference which dealt with policy, that Mr. Nash wanted, in committee, to wipe out that portion of our banking and currency policy which says "until the State is the sole authority for the issue of credit and currency," but that policy was again re-affirmed by last Conference, was contained in statements and in the manifesto to the people, and it is our duty to see that it is given effect to. Anything in the nature of increasing the interest rate for the purpose of raising an internal loan at the present moment will mean that the forces we defeated during the election have won a battle inside the Party they could not win on the Hustings. I do not think we will throw in the towel like that after emerging with a majority of well over 100,000. There must be no increase in the interest rate. There can be none without betrayal.

This letter may seem rather extraordinary but I am concerned by the nature of the crisis as never in my life, and I set greater store by the things in which I believe than in the job which I happen to hold or the opinions others may have of me. I have no confidence in Mr. Nash's handling of any financial problem, I never have had. Mr. Nash knows I have not, for I have not concealed my opinion, and as one man I am entitled to that opinion. In November, 1935, after the Party had been successful, I wrote a brief letter to the Prime Minister in which I had the audacity to say that in my opinion Mr. Nash as an administrator, as a codifier, had such capacity that the Prime Minister could give him 50 per cent of the portfolios, but I went on to say that he had such reverence for the orthodox financial system that I trusted that he would not be made Minister of Finance, as if he were, within three years every militant element in the Party would be up against the Minister of Finance. I believed then that the Prime Minister himself would take the Finance portfolio; I said so in that letter. As it was, the Prime Minister became responsible for his colleague instead of for his own opinions. No doubt my courage was held in evidence against me for only "yes" men are preferred. I think it is true to say that Mr. Nash's orthodoxy would have put us out of office had Caucus not been repeatedly successful in forcing his hand. For instance, Mr. Nash did not want an invalidity pension in the first year of our office. Some members of Cabinet may have wanted it but Cabinet generally supported Mr. Nash, under the mistaken assumption of loyalty to Cabinet instead of to principle. Caucus did want an invalidity pension and forced the position. Mr. Nash wanted old-age pensions to be increased by half-a-crown only, and it will be remembered that the Prime Minister refused to accept from Caucus a resolution to increase pensions by a further half-a-crown, again I believe, inspired by loyalty to his Minister and not to his sentiments. The resolution was moved at a later Caucus, was opposed by members of the Cabinet present, Mr. Langstone supporting Caucus, but when the intention of the overwhelming majority of Caucus was shown, the resolution was carried out without a vote against it.

We had the increase in the refunding loan from 3¼ per cent, to 3½ per cent, sponsored by Mr. Nash after a Reserve Bank Board decision that 3½ per cent should be the rate. But the original decision to re-borrow ALL the necessary money was a disavowal of our pledges re debt anyhow.

We had Mr. Nash's letters telling local bodies to hypothecate their debentures to private banks—a distinct disavowal of our policy.

Although Mr. Nash is to be Minister of Social Security, his was the greatest opposition to the present Social Security Scheme. Mr. Nash

Opposing the Money Lenders

proposed a Social Security Scheme which really was an alternative to our financial policy, i.e., we were to raise the necessary funds for Public Development by a compulsory wage cut of 7½ per cent, or 1s 6d in the £, which amount was to be used to build up a huge investment fund. The wealthiest people in New Zealand were to get their 7 1/2 per cent returned at a certain age, plus the interest earned, a complete breaking-down of the Labour party's financial ideas. And for the compulsory wage cut of 2½ per cent, present pensioners were to receive no increment. There was to be no medical care and attention, and the pension was only to be available at 65 instead of 60.

Mr. Nash set up his extraordinary Dairy Company of reactionaries, thereby losing us the butter seat

Mr. Nash opposed the taking over of the Bank of New Zealand.

Mr. Nash resisted exchange control until he has no alternative except to default, and delay has endangered the welfare of all the people we represent.

Little effort indeed except grudgingly and under pressure has been made to give effect to Labour's financial policy. Nor will any effort be made so long as our financial policy is controlled by refractory instruments who do not believe in the policy's practicability.

It is with regret that I address this letter to members of Caucus, but a crisis has arisen of staggering importance, due to the shilly-shallying and drift engaged in to date. And further crises will arise. A Labour Party confronted with great opportunity cannot allow itself to be indefinitely kept from doing the right thing by a refractory dictatorship. If we fail, the people of New Zealand who have trusted us will be the ones to suffer. If we fail, our failure will re-echo around the world. The test is not what we have done, but have we done what it was and is our power to do. We must advance boldly and in the light of our principles and ideals. The Party at the moment reminds me of a person advancing on the battlefield and who, confronted with a machine-gun wants to take time off to consider whether he should have enlisted or not. Even if he runs he will be shot. The best chance is forward in the way of our faith and promises.

I know that having written this statement I shall be accused of wrecking and malingering and desiring to assassinate, but the statement is written because of a desire to see Labour succeed because of its adherence to principles. I still think that the best way to win the people of New Zealand is to be courageous in regard to the things that we promised and to go straight ahead; and I personally am prepared to incur any additional unpopularity within the Party at the expense of expressing my viewpoint, rather than sit in silence while the Labour Movement is allowed to bungle on to disaster with people who vacillate on the bridge.

Mr. Nash led Caucus recently to believe that he favoured borrowing in New Zealand at higher rates of interest. Maybe we are already paying 4 per cent to the Reserve Bank because we are allowing finance to dictate policy to us. Indeed, in this morning's paper I read a statement from Mr. Nash that the Government proposes to issue an internal loan to meet capital expenditure in connection with railway and electrical equipment and other public works. If the loan is an external one for the purpose of buying machinery that we have not got in New Zealand, no objection can be taken; but if it is proposed to raise money in New Zealand for further internal development, it is a flagrant disavowal of the Labour Party's policy. It means that after having won two elections, pledged to win New Zealand freedom from privately controlled finance, we are agreeing to perpetuate the borrowing system and to increase interest rates for money unobtainable at 3 1/4 per cent. I am afraid I for one cannot swallow my words and my principles quite so easily, and I know this is true of most of the Party. It would be an act of cowardice on my part if I failed to protest, as well as the definite betrayal of the Labour Movement I happen to represent in the Parliament of New Zealand. We have just emerged from an election with a majority for the second time, and the moment is now opportune to try the Labour way instead of the Nash way.

I cannot address Caucus verbally regarding my ideas of the dangers of the present public announcement what we intend to perpetuate the private borrowing system which means an increase in interest rates, because of the existing "lock-out", so I must address you in this statement.

To perpetuate the borrowing process is to sell the people of New Zealand. To increase the internal interest rate instead of positively reducing the internal interest rate is to sell the people of New Zealand. The time has arrived when all members should express their viewpoint for the purpose of safeguarding the interests of the Movement they are pledged to support, for it is a Movement, a set of principles, and not merely a refractory instrument of the Labour Party, to which we owe our loyalty.

Opposing the Money Lenders

It is as well to realise that it is the way in which finance policy has been practically dictated by Mr. Nash that is at the real basis of the present dispute in the Party. When members move to elect Cabinet, they move to try to get some power to endeavour to cause Mr. Nash to team with rather than dictate to the majority. I have a lot of faith in the commonsense of my colleagues, and however sincerely I may hold a viewpoint I am prepared to set aside my opinion if the majority determine that we should go some other way. But it is intolerable that the majority should have little say and should be compelled to go the way of Mr. Nash. We shall achieve comradeship once more when all important policy issues are determined by majority vote.

COME ON, THE GREEN SHIRTS!

**HOW TO ORGANISE
THE
GREEN SHIRT
MOVEMENT
FOR
SOCIAL CREDIT
IN
YOUR DISTRICT**

John Hargrave's "Green Shirts"

John Hargrave

In 1935 the poet Ezra Pound, a seminal influence on modern English literature, and also a tireless proponent of Social Credit as the means by which the distorting factor of money on culture could be overthrown, dedicated *Social Credit: An Impact*, to 'the Green Shirts of England'. The Green Shirts were among the most militant of those in the Anglophone world fighting the money-changers amidst the Great Depression, and the travesty of 'poverty amidst plenty'. Britain's Green Shirts were probably only matched in their crusading militancy by Canada's Pilgrims of Saint Michael, and Father Charles Coughlin's National Union for Social Justice in the USA. While these latter two were motivated by Catholic social doctrine and the papal encyclicals against usury, the British Green Shirts were inspired by a different heritage.

White Fox

The Green Shirts grew from the Woodcraft movement of Baden Powell's Boy Scouts. John Hargrave, or White Fox, his nom de plume in Scouting journals, was a 26 year old war veteran and Commissioner for Woodcraft and Camping in Baden Powell's movement when he and other Scout masters formed the Kindred of the Kibbo Kift. The term derives from archaic Kentish, meaning 'a proof of great strength'. The movement was inspired by Medievalism and the Saxon heritage. Folkmoots and Althings were organised in heathen tradition. Training included woodcraft, the forming of craft guilds, cultural development and the use of ritual of Norse and Saxon type. Kinsmen were organised into Clans and Tribes. The Kibbo Kift uniform was handmade by the wearer or by a 'rooftree' (family group).

Hargave's experiences as a sergeant with the stretcher-bearers in the world war (he was at the time a pacifist from a Quaker family) led to his belief that civilisation had failed and that only a few individuals could recreate themselves by withdrawing from corrupt industrial society. One can see the raison d'etre of Kibbo Kift with its harking back to pre-industrial and pre-capitalist English society to reinstall values that were beyond materialism and realigned with nature and the folk. The moral, social, political, and economic crises of the world war had evoked a similar movement across Germany in the Wandervogel of young people who hiked through the country, singing as they went and forging a new form of camaraderie. Indeed, there were contacts between the two. Hargrave's woodcraft books had been translated into German, and Kinsmen attended Wandervogel camps.

Hargrave had originally eschewed politics. However his movement began to attract socialists, and he was resistant to their ideology. At the 1924 Althing a socialist faction attempted to take over. Hargrave gave them ten minutes to pack up and get out. A small number left to form the Woodcraft Folk.

Social Credit

Employed as a draughtsman for an advertising agency, in 1923 Hargrave was introduced by the agency to Major C. H. Douglas, whose series of articles in *The New Age*, the journal of the guild-socialist literary figure A. R. Orage, resulted in the Social Credit theory. Orage, like some other Fabian-socialists, was an unorthodox socialist, and believed in a return to the guilds as a higher form of unionism. He saw in Douglas' theory the means of eliminating the rule of the money-power. It was from here that literary figures such as Ezra Pound, T. S. Elliot, and the New Zealand poet A. R. D. Fairburn were attracted to Social Credit as the means of freeing humanity from debt-bondage and creating a new society in which culture would flourish once the arts were no longer treated as commodities.

In this vein, while Kibbo Kift enabled its members to devote themselves to a life as individuals cleansed of the corruption of industrial civilisation by harking back to a pre-capitalist ethos, Hargrave et al saw that Social Credit could free the whole of society. Hargrave wrote: 'Half our problem is psychological and the other half is economic. The psychological complex of industrial mankind can only be released by solving the economic impasse'. By 1927 most of the Kibbo Kift leaders had been converted, and a Social Credit plank was added to their principles.

In 1930 the Legion of the Unemployed was established in Coventry. In 1931 the legion adopted a military style green shirt and beret. Soon the Legion was affiliated to Hargrave's movement as the Green Shirts

Opposing the Money Lenders

of Kibbo Kift. At the annual Kindfest of January 1931 Hargrave stated that it was the duty of Kibbo Kift to break the power of the 'money mongers'. This could not be done by party politics but by a movement to show the people 'that absolute, that religious, that military devotion to duty without which no great cause was ever brought to a successful issue'. In 1932 Kibbo Kift adopted the green shirt uniform, and the name was changed to the Green Shirt Movement for Social Credit.

Hargrave advocated a new strategy. Social Credit until then had been quietly discussed in study groups and written of in journals of limited circulation. A militant campaign would break the silent treatment of the press, and take the issue to the streets, with marches, street corner meetings, banners and drums, publicity stunts and tabloid newspapers. Major Douglas gave the movement his approval. These were rough times. A genteel approach would be squashed by the Communists, as Sir Oswald Mosley had learned when he broke with the Labour Party and formed the New Party, soon after founding the black-shirted British Union of Fascists to meet Communist violence, the same year that the Green Shirts were established in 1932.

Green Shirts on the March

With opposition from both the news media and the Communists, the Green Shirts were noted for their discipline and order in the face of provocation. They joined or organised hunger marches and demonstrations by the unemployed workers' movement.

On 9 June 1932 the first open air meeting of the Green Shirts was held in Lewisham High Street. From then until October 1934, 3,426 open air meetings and 32 demonstrations were held, 56,000 newspapers sold, and 223,000 leaflets distributed. From 1933 through to 1937 the movement's newspaper *Attack* was published. Something of the character of the movement can be discerned from the year 1934 for example:

May 16: Deputation to the Bank of England and to Downing Street.

June 27: A green painted brick was thrown through the window of 11 Downing Street, residence of the Chancellor of the Exchequer. (The green painted brick and the green arrow were symbols of the movement, the minor vandalism resulting in court action that enabled publicity for Social Credit ideas).

John Hargrave

July 4: Lord Straboli received a deputation of Green Shirts and he raised the question of the National Dividend in the House of Lords.

November 5: Deputation to P.C. Loftus Member of Parliament, at the House of Commons.

In 1935 the movement became the Social Credit Party of Great Britain and Northern Ireland. Other features of the movement's campaign during the pre-war years included:

1935: General Election, W. Townsend received 11.01% at South Leeds.

November 1936: Hargrave travelled to Alberta and was appointed economic adviser by the new Social Credit government, where he draws up the Hargrave Plan.

January 1937: Public Order Act bans political uniforms.

October 1937: 'Hands off Alberta' painted in green on the Bank of England building.

February 1938: green painted brick thrown through the window of the Bank of Montreal, Threadneedle Street, in solidarity with the Alberta Government.

March 1938: the first shout of 'Social Credit the only remedy' is heard from the public gallery of the House of Commons. This became a frequent occurrence.

1938: May Day demonstrations with green shirts hoisted on to poles, in protest against the banning of the uniform. Green bricks thrown at 10 Downing Street.

July 1938: there is a falling-out with Major Douglas at a Chiltern Court meeting.

October 1938: Coventry petition to the King demanding an enquiry into the money system.

Guy Fawkes Day 1938 an effigy of Montagu Norman, Governor of the Bank of England, burnt outside the bank.

January 1938: sheaf of wheat burnt outside a meeting of the Wheat

Opposing the Money Lenders

Commission, with the slogan, 'they burn the wheat we want to eat.' This is a reference to 'poverty amidst plenty' when farmers were paid to destroy crops and livestock during the Great Depression.

April 1939: 'conscript the bankers first' demonstrations in London.

Despite the difficulties caused by World War II, with many members called up to service, the movement continued its campaign:

February 1940: 'Robin Hood' wearing the illegal green shirt shoots a green arrow at 10 Downing Street.

March 1940: effigy of Montagu Norman burned at the entrance of the Bank of England (offender sentenced to three months hard labour).

April 1940 a woman wearing a green crinoline dress – 'out of date, like the money system' – protests to the Chancellor of the Exchequer.

May 1942: 'Britain can feed herself' campaign launched.

During this time Hargrave had published his novel *Summer Time Ends* (1935) on mass apathy and the corrupt system. In 1937 he invented an automatic navigation system for aircraft. In 1939 he published a novel based on the Governor of the Bank of England, the omnipotent Montagu Norman. The Bank responded by buying up and destroying every copy of the book. In 1938 he started the fortnightly *Message from Hargrave*, which ran to 1951.

After The War

With the end of the war, the Social Credit Party was reactivated, and a Social Credit Envangel was formed.

December 1945: A 'Britannia' demonstration against the Bretton Woods Agreement that established the World Bank and the International Monetary Fund as the basis for the post-war world economic system.

January 1946: Publication of *Social Credit Clearly Explained*.

July 1946: 'Down with bread rationing' demonstration.

June 1947: Banner demonstration at Epsom Derby.

John Hargrave

August 1947: Banner demonstration at the Oval Test Match.

May 1948: First post-war assembly of the Social Credit Party.

November 1949: Hargrave speaks to 5000 senior citizens at Central Hall, Westminster.

February 1950: General Election, Hargrave wins 550 votes at Stoke Newington and Hackney.

November 1950: First of eight monthly shouts of 'Social Credit the only remedy' from the public gallery at Parliament.

Despite the constant activism, mass apathy reigned in the post-war world. After a poor showing of votes in April 1951 for Hargrave, the Social Credit Party was dissolved.

Hargrave enjoyed much success as a novelist after the war. He was acclaimed when he attended a 1976 performance of a stage musical about the Green Shirts in 1976.

In 1977 the Kibbo Kift Foundation was formed with Hargrave as chairman, to preserve the archives and regalia of the movement. Much of Hargrave's energies were taken up with showing that he was the inventor of the automatic navigation system widely used on aircraft, including Concorde. He was eventually accorded grudging recognition but was denied compensation on a technicality. He died on 21 November 1982. The Social Credit Party was re-established in 1965 by C. J. Hunt, a member of the original Hargarve party, but was disbanded in 1978.

Social Credit Clearly Explained

1. What is the Increment of Association which Social Credit People Talk About?

Ten men together—in association—can do what ten men separately cannot do. The outcome of such work-in-association is the ' increment of association'—that is: Real Wealth (goods and services) produced by working together, instead of each man alone.

In a modern Power-Age community every individual is entitled to his fair share of the 'increment of association', even if his or her quota of work is not needed in the Productive System. That is because the Productive System is able to produce enough and to spare for all, and if it is not taken up and used it will have to be scrapped—or Production cut down—which is absurd. Social Credit makes it possible to distribute a fair share of the 'increment of association' to everyone by means of a National Dividend.

2. What are 'The Wages of the Machine' That Social Credit People Talk About?

They are the wages that would have been paid to human beings if machinery and improved processes had not made their labour partially or wholly unnecessary. Under the present Work-Wage System, human beings released from the Productive System are left practically without buying- power except for a miserable 'dole'. In the past these people have been called 'The Unemployed.'

The Social Credit National Dividend is, in reality, the 'Wages of the Machine' that will enable the unemployed, and everyone else, to take up and use the goods and services produced with less and less human labour.

3. Isn't Social Credit a 'Something for Nothing' Scheme?

What makes you think a 'something for nothing' scheme is wrong? When the Sun shines upon the Earth there is no charge on the stream of Solar Energy we receive. It comes to us free of charge. It is something for nothing. Yet without this stream of Solar Energy there would be no life of any kind on this planet--not so much as a blade of grass!

Solar Energy is God's gift to man, Social Credit is a method for allowing God's gift to man to be used—in the form of goods and services—by everyone.

4. But Surely it is Impossible to get 'Something for Nothing?'

That is nonsense, and it is Bankers' nonsense. I have just stated, in answer to the foregoing question, that the whole of Creation is, in fact, a something-for-nothing scheme. It is perfectly possible to get ' something for nothing'. You do it every moment of the day, when you breathe the air, and when you see with your eyes by the light of the sun.

It is quite true that you cannot get 'something from nothing' nor can matter be changed from one form to another without expending energy—but that is totally different. We are not proposing to attempt to get something from nothing. We are proposing to take and use Real Wealth, which is a product of Solar Energy.

5. Does Plenty Really Exist?

In normal peacetime it certainly does. Have a look at the items listed in answer to Question 6, Were Consumable Goods that could have been used Really Destroyed on a Large Scale?

'If an engineer dictator over industry could be appointed, and given complete control over raw materials, machinery and trained labour; he could flood, smother and bury the people under an avalanche of goods and services such as not Utopian dreamer ever imagined.'—Ralph E. Flanders, President of the American Society of Mechanical Engineers, in 1937.

6. Were Consumable Goods That Could Have Been Used Really Destroyed on a Large Scale?

Here is a mere fraction of the record of deliberate destruction as published in the Press:-

- 'Enormous sabotage of food supplies by allowing 2,500,000 acres of English arable land to go out of cultivation between 1919 and 1930. "Bumper Wheat Crops in Canada-Crushing Blow to Markets."' (*Daily Herald*, 1932.)

Opposing the Money Lenders

- 'Sugar position" improved" by destruction in Cuba.' (*Daily Express*, 1932)
- 'Holland destroyed 100,000 pigs.' (*Evening News*, 1932.)
- 'Hurricane "helps" sugar position in Cuba.' (*Daily Express*, 1932.)
- 'Portugal destroyed 10,000,000 gallons of wine.' (*Daily Express*, 1932.)
- 'France " welcomed mildew" to reduce wine output.' (*Evening Standard*, 1932.)
- 'Holland burnt 15,000,000 flower bulbs.' (*Sunday Pictorial*, 1932.)
- 'Irish beer poured into the gutter.' (*Times*, 1932.)
- 'Russian failure of wheat crops " brings better prospects." ' (*Daily Express*, 1933.)
- 'France fines farmers for increasing acreage.' (*Times*, 1933.)
- '2,000,000 tons of sugar "withheld from market."' (1933.)
- 'U.S.A., ploughs in 25 per cent of cotton crop.' (*Evening News*, 1933.)
- 'Up to the middle of September, 1933, approximately 22,250,000,000 acres of coffee had been thrown into the sea, burnt, and made into briquettes and used as fuel.' (*Daily Herald*, 1933.)
- 'U.S.A, destroyed 2,000,000 sows, and 4,000,000 little pigs.' (*New Democracy*, 1933.)
- 'International plan for destruction of cocoa.' (*Evening News*, 1933.)
- 'British farmers forced to kill cattle too soon.' (*Daily Express*, 1933.)
- '225,000 sheep slaughtered.' (Observer, 1933.)
- 'Herring glut threatens starvation.' (*Daily Express*, 1933.)
- '60,000 sheep slaughtered and burnt in San Julian area, Argentine.' (1933.)
- 'Denmark incinerated 25,000 cattle.' (*Sphere*, 1933.)
- 'Canada, Argentine, and U.S.A. worried about " too much bread" in 1936.' (*Daily Express*, 1933.)

- 'Innumerable schemes for restriction of wheat acreage.' (*Daily Express*, 1933.)
- 'Stoking railway engines with wheat in Canada.' (*Star*, 1934.)
- 'Southend sells fish for manure.' (*Daily Mirror*, 1934.)
- 'Brazil destroys over 26,000,000 bags of coffee.' (*Evening Standard*, 1934.)
- 'Too much corn—Government hint at reduction plan.' (*Daily Express*, 1934.)
- 'Scottish farmer dumping his potato crop into the sea.' (Star, 1934.)
- '5,000 lambs driven into the sea and drowned in New Zealand' (*Sydney Sun*, 1933.)
- 'U.S.A. ploughs in every third row of cotton' (*New Democracy*, 1933.)
- '250,000 cwt. of hops destroyed, worth £2,000,000' (*Daily Herald*, 1934.)
- '£15,000 in fines collected from potato growers for exceeding the acreage allowed by the Potato Marketing Board' (*Daily Express*, 1935.)
- 'Stornoway fishing fleet struck heavy shoals of fish on three successive days. Market glutted. About 1,700 crans sold at prices ranging from 19/- to 33/-. Samples representing another 1,500 crans lying on market floor without an offer.' (*Daily Express*, 1935.)

That was in the 'locust years' before the Hitler war. But even in war-time, with the whole nation fighting for its very existence, its food drastically rationed, and compelled to rely mainly upon home-grown supplies, many instances of deliberate food destruction—especially fish—were reported in the Press.

14. How Will the Budget Be Calculated?

A Taxation Budget will not be required, but a Real Wealth Budget showing National Production (plus Imports) and National Consumption (plus Exports) will be drawn up, presented to Parliament, and made known to the public. In reality, it will be a National Stocksheet, showing in terms of cost-values how much has been added to the nation's wealth, and how much subtracted, during a given period.

Opposing the Money Lenders

The first will always exceed the second (except for a natural catastrophe), and so there will always be a surplus over the accounting period; and this, after the Government's consumption has been subtracted. So the old-style 'problem' of 'balancing the Budget' will be turned upside down. Instead of requiring the collection of taxes to recover a deficit, it will require the distribution of a National Dividend to dispose of a surplus.

Here is a specimen of a Real Credit Budget, drawn up by A. L. Gibson, Fellow of the Institute of Chartered Accountants, and a Social Credit advocate. Please bear in mind that the figures in this specimen are merely token-figures to illustrate the method of drawing up such a budget:-

At convenient intervals—quarterly, half-yearly, or yearly—a Social Credit Government will have prepared a REAL CREDIT BUDGET.

18. Who Will Be Entitled to Draw the National Dividend And Will It be Paid to Children?

Every individual who is legally recognised as a British subject and who has lived in Britain for, say, two years or more, should be entitled to draw the National Dividend.

It will probably not be paid directly to children. Some arrangement might be made whereby it could be drawn, if required, by the parents or guardians, to be expended for the benefit of the child until the legal age is reached, which may be fixed at the school-leaving age. Thereafter, the child will be entitled to draw its own National Dividend. If not drawn by the parents or guardians, the child will be credited with the yearly amount in the Post Office or bank (i.e., Local Credit Office) and it can be drawn as a lump sum, or as required, by the child upon reaching the legal age, Thereafter, the child, now growing to manhood or womanhood, can draw the National Dividend as an adult.

To be born into the world with Real Wealth waiting for you (instead of being born in Debt) may seem strange to us, but in certain African tribes where goats are 'money', the tribe as a whole sets aside a certain number of goats when a child is born, so that it shall have a share of the tribal wealth to start with.

If ignorant (?) and poverty-stricken (?) savages (?) can provide for their children in this way, surely a highly cultured, civilized community, with all the advantages of modern science, should be able to do so far more?

19. Will Inherited Incomes Continue plus the National Dividend?

At the outset inherited incomes will continue plus the National Dividend, if people inheriting such incomes choose to draw the Dividend. But the whole practice of 'Wills and Bequests' will tend to die out, along with all other forms of saving or hoarding.

People save money and leave it in their wills to their descendants (a) from a fear of poverty in the future, and (b) in order to show how 'successful' they have been! This tendency to save and leave money will gradually disappear in a Social Credit State. It will look, and be, unnecessary and foolish, because everyone will have an ' inherited income'—the National Dividend—based upon the Cultural Inheritance and Increment of Association of past and present generations. Instead of 'amassing wealth' and then leaving it to someone else, people will tend to spend their money while they are alive, knowing that their descendants will be adequately provided for by the National Dividend.

20. Will a Millionaire Receive the National Dividend?

Yes, if he chooses to draw it. Why not? There is plenty for all. But if not, he will in any case benefit by the price-discount. 'Oh, so under Social Credit there will still be millionaires?' I hear someone say.

Under Social Credit everyone—including millionaires—will have a birthright income (the National Dividend) based on the productive capacity of the total community. Under Capitalism the millionaires are a tiny fraction of the total population, and under Social Credit this tiny millionaire-class will tend to disappear as the National Dividend increases with production. Why? Because a man who is assured of a birthright income that can meet his needs from day to day, and who has no fear of the future, will not bother his head to amass a fortune. The 'get rich quick' incentive will lose its force, and as the power of money is reduced by the Social Credit technique, so the desire to accumulate it will fade away.

Opposing the Money Lenders

21. *How Will You Fix and Control Prices?*

Prices will not be 'fixed', they will be adjusted. This means that they will rise and fall with the production of goods and services.

22. *Will Not Social Credit Lead to Inflation?*

No, how can it? The Social Credit method of issuing any new consumer buying-power is always accompanied by a fall in prices.

If prices are falling, how can they (at the same time) be rising?

In other words: how can there be inflation if, instead of rising, prices are falling? Those who assert that 'Social Credit would lead to inflation' must answer this question logically, or admit that their inflation fears are groundless. Never yet has there been a logical answer to this question from the critics of Social Credit. Always they conveniently ignore the working of the Price Adjustment—which is the vital mechanism of Social Credit.

By means of the two-fold synchromeshed mechanism of National-Dividend and Price Adjustment, inflation is absolutely impossible.

23. *How Exactly Will the National Dividend Be Cancelled?*

It will be cancelled when you pay it to a retailer in exchange for goods or services. After that it is cancelled right through the system. It is then no longer consumer buying power. The process is as follows:

1. The Retailer, to keep solvent, must use it to pay the Wholesaler, retaining only an agreed profit, i.e., his service fee.

2. The Wholesaler, to keep solvent, must use it to pay the Producer, retaining only his agreed profit or service fee.

3. The Producer, to keep solvent, must use it to pay production costs, retaining only his agreed profit or service fee.

24. *Won't a Social Credit State Suffer From Lack of Imports?*

No. On condition that it produces a Real Export Surplus, it will be able to get all necessary imports from abroad.

25. How Will a Social Credit Britain Pay for Necessary Imports?

By exporting its Real Surplus—i.e., goods not needed in the Home Market—via;

(a) a National Import-Export Clearing House, and calculating the transaction in financial terms, the goods imported from abroad in return for this Real Export Surplus will be sold in Great Britain at the Scientific Price then prevailing.

The money-payments for imports will be made by credits received from other countries for our Real Export Surplus.

As the Real Export Surplus will consist of goods not required by the Home Market, they can be sold abroad at any price whatever.

No policy of 'dumping' would be necessary, however, because (a) non- Social-Credit countries must find export markets, while

(b) a Social Credit World would have no difficulty in arranging the exchange of Real Surpluses both of raw materials and finished goods via an International Import-Export Clearing House.

28. Suppose Other Countries Refuse to Trade on That Basis, and Demand Gold?

That is a form of financial blackmail that no Social Credit State will tolerate. Its method of resisting such financial pressure will be to cease to trade with any country attempting to apply such pressure. The result will be the loss to that country of 'a valuable export market', while the Social Credit State will not suffer so heavily, since it is not dependent (financially) upon export markets. The corresponding loss of imports to the Social Credit State will only be serious in the case of ' essential raw materials'—and the Hitler war has shown that apart from war production, very few raw materials from abroad are absolutely essential to the maintenance of life and health in the British Isles. In other words: a stop-all-exports-to-Britain campaign could not succeed in either starving us out or bringing our productive system to a standstill.

The fact that all non-Social Credit countries are compelled by their financial debt-system to 'export or die' will make them think twice and three times before attempting a no-goods-for-Britain policy. Any such attempt will compel the non-exporting country to (a) find some other export market; or (b) to destroy part of its goods for export; or (c) distribute them to its own consumers—which can only be done by making its own Home Market effective by applying Social Credit principles.

Thus, the attempt to boycott or starve-out a Social Credit State by depriving it of imports, is certain to drive the ' boycotter' towards Social Credit--simply because, under the debt-system of orthodox finance, it must 'export or die'. Foreign Manufacturers of goods for export will certainly not welcome any decree banning exports, unless their goods can be sold at an economic price in the Home Market--and this can only be done by financing the consumer in accordance with the Social Credit technique.

Social Credit established in any one country will, therefore, tend to drive all other countries towards Social Credit; and the threat of a ban on exports will automatically speed-up the process.

30. How Will a Social Credit Britain Deal with Post-War Europe?

If Britain is in a position to bring effective pressure to bear upon post-war Europe, two things must be insisted upon:

1. A Debt free Peace—the cancellation of all war-debts.

2. The establishment of a Debt-free Europe operating a financially costless system of exchange in each country in accordance with the Social Credit technique of national accountancy. That is: a Social Credit Europe.

Frontier problems should not be dealt with until after each country has established its own Social Credit economy. Questions as to where one country ends and another begins are not vital questions in a Continental Community operating Social Credit. For a time frontiers could be fluid and, indeed, under Social Credit the frontiers of post-war Europe would tend to become of no more importance than the county boundaries in Britain to-day.

John Hargrave

What Will Social Credit Do?

31. How Will Social Credit Put a Stop to War?

By cutting out the chief cause of war—the international scramble for Export Markets.

The nations of the world are compelled, under the present Bankers' Debt system, to compete with each other for Export Markets, because, under this system, they cannot make their Home Markets effective. This is the root of all modern war.

Social Credit makes the Home Market effective, and by abolishing needless Poverty at home, avoids War abroad.

32. Surely Wars Are Produced by Far More Than Merely Economic Causes?

Why do you use the word 'merely'? Without Food, Warmth, Shelter, you cannot remain alive. A careful examination of the history of mankind shows that most wars, among the more primitive peoples as among the so-called 'civilised' are caused by pressure of economic circumstances, no matter what the high-sounding 'excuse' may be for going to war. There can be no doubt whatever that the main cause of all modern war is the scramble for export markets. People are told that they are fighting for ' freedom' , and indeed they are fighting for freedom to live. There can be no freedom to live under the present financial debt-system without 'freedom' (an outlet) for exports. When the Dictators said, 'Expand or explode' , ' Export or die', they were merely repeating what the Democratic Governments proclaim when they say, 'We cannot live without exports'. This is the seething cauldron of war, and it is no use speaking of 'merely economic' causes as though these were not the main causes. Almost all the impulses towards war are the outcome of these economic causes. To deal with the impulses arising, is to deal with the symptoms of the disease and not with the root cause of it.

33. Does Social Credit Make a Clean Sweep of Capitalism Or Does it Preserve Some Part of the Old System and So Keep Capitalism Going?

Capitalism is a system of production without an adequate mechanism of distribution, Social Credit will establish an effective mechanism of distribution that will enable everyone to have a

Opposing the Money Lenders

fair share of the goods and services that are, in fact, efficiently produced by the so-called 'capitalist system'.

It is no use trying to maintain that the so-called 'capitalist system' does not produce goods and services efficiently. It does. You have only to look in the shops and showrooms to convince yourself about this. There you will see the actual finished products of 'capitalist' manufacture.

You will see chairs, tables, beds, carpets, curtains, clothing, knives, forks, spoons, cups, saucers, plates, motor-cars, radios, vacuum cleaners, refrigerators, electric irons, lamps, radiators, kettles and a thousand and one other things.

It is quite ridiculous to suggest that these things are not made efficiently by the so-called 'capitalist system'. Go into the shops, buy what you want and take it home, and you will find that these capitalist-produced articles are well constructed, useful, and sometimes even beautiful.

The truth is that the main problem of Production has been solved by 'capitalism' but your problem of being able to go into the shops and get what you want has not been solved. It is a money problem, not a problem of production.

Social Credit will solve this money problem. In doing so it abolishes the exploitation of the Many by the Few, which is the malignant disease of the banker-ridden 'capitalist system', by giving everyone a birthright income- the National Dividend—that no one can suspend, stop, nor interfere with it in any way. It does not keep Capitalism going. It transforms Capitalism and turns it into Social Credit. Therefore it makes a clean sweep of Capitalism.

34. What Will Happen to the Bank of England and the Banks Generally?

The Bank of England will become the Credit Issue Department of the National Credit Office, and the Bank will become, in effect, branches of the National Credit Office, They will take up their proper function in a modern Power-Age society as the National Book-keeping Organisation of the whole community.

They will be required by law to operate the Social Credit technique under the central authority of the National Credit Office. For this service to the community they will, of course, be paid an agreed service fee.

The actual property-ownership of bank buildings, etc., is of no particular importance, just as the scales and yard measure of every little retail shop throughout the country must conform to the requirements of the Weights and Measures Act, and does in fact conform without being 'nationalised', so the Bank of England and the Banks generally w ill carry out the requirements of a National Credit (Equation of Consumption to Production) Act.

A Parliamentary Bill setting forth the necessary clauses has already been drafted by the Social Credit Party of Great Britain.

35. *What Will Happen to the Stock Exchange and Investments?*

Nothing, so far as a Social Credit Government is concerned so long as no attempt is made to create a 'scare' or to stampede the public into a 'financial panic'. People who own a part of a business must always be entitled to dispose of their share to someone else, but as price levels will be predictable over long periods, the Stock Exchange will lose its attraction for gamblers and will become once again a place where stocks can be exchanged.

As the main incentive to invest money will tend to 'evaporate' by the introduction of Social Credit, and as the chief business of the Stock Exchange is the buying and selling of stocks and shares for customers, this institution is certain to become obsolete in the long run. It w ill not be needed. When everyone is assured of the National Dividend, the incentive to speculate, or gamble, on the Stock Exchange, will die out.

As regards foreign dealings, its place will be taken by the Import-Export Clearing House Department of the National Credit Office.

Regarding investments: the dividends drawn from them will, under Social Credit, buy more goods and services, but the inducement to invest i.e., to secure an unearned income—will gradually die away as financial security becomes the rule and not the exception.

As any new enterprise that is wanted by the community will be financed by new credits from the National Credit Office, the field for ordinary investments will narrow. There will, however, remain spheres in which personal savings can be used to promote new ventures, and people will naturally be free to finance and own businesses created by themselves or their associates.

37. What About Taxation?

Taxation is the raising of a revenue from members of a community by the imposition of compulsory contributions, usually in the form of money. The term taxation covers every conceivable exaction that a government can make, whether under the name of a tax, or under such names as rates, assessments, duties, imposts, excise, licences, fees, tolls, etc.

The purpose of taxation is to raise a revenue with which to pay for government and other public services, because, under the bankers' Debt-system, the Government has no money—i.e., the community is deemed to have no power to create its own public credit for these purposes, and can only carry on by (a) taxing itself by taking away a proportion of its buying-power which cannot then be spent on consumer goods, or (b) borrowing its own credit-power from the bankers, which again means taxing itself in order to pay interest and/or pay back the sum borrowed.

A Social Credit Government will not need revenue from taxation (i.e., buying-power taken from your pocket), nor will it have to borrow one farthing from the Bankers, because the money needed for all government and other public services will be public (debt-free) credit issued by the National Credit Office for these purposes, based upon the actual productive capacity of the whole community. Therefore, under Social Credit, all forms of taxation will tend to fall into disuse, and finally there will be no taxation of any kind.

Under the ramshackle Heath Robinson mechanism of the Bankers' Debt- system, taxation is a method—a very crude method—of regulating the amount of buying-power in the hands of the community. Under Social Credit this will be automatically regulated by the operation of the Scientific Price Adjustment at the retail end.

39. Will Social Credit Provide Full Employment?

It places no obstacle in the way of full employment, if that is the will of the people. It does warn them, however, that such an objective means that men must replace The Machine, which in time means that the output of goods will dwindle towards zero.

Providing employment is not the objective of a sane social-economic system. A sane social-economic system must give economic security with as much individual freedom and leisure as possible. Social Credit does this by means of the National Dividend and Price Adjustment. The object is not 'full employment'—but full enjoyment. Not at all the same thing, in spite of what moralists tell us.

40. If Everyone Gets a National Dividend Will Anyone Do Any Work?

If they don't, there won't be any National Dividend.

The National Dividend is based upon the production of Real Wealth (goods and services), and will rise and fall with production. No Production-no Dividend!

47. Will People Know What to Do With Their Leisure?

Well, will YOU know what to do with yours? After all, there are plenty of things to do in the world, and it will not take most people long to find out what they are once they have time to do so. (Some people may like to go fishing. It doesn't interest me but every man to his own choice....)

What 'you may ask, will people do with their leisure?'

To begin with, of course, there will not be much leisure, because there is such an enormous amount of reconstruction to be done. For ten years at least, after this war, there will be work for all. We have to re-shape our world. But, all the same, we must re-shape it in such a way as to establish a Leisure State in a Power Age. If we don't, we shall be heading straight for World War III.

Quite gradually people will come to value their leisure because it will allow them time to 'work' at work of their own choosing. It will give them freedom to work at work worth doing. No more 'square pegs in round holes'.

Opposing the Money Lenders

Released from a great deal of industrial drudgery, people will begin to take up a thousand and one activities, and in a Leisure State we shall find the majority of people working harder than ever!—but at work they have chosen, want to do, and enjoy.

Have no fear: a Social Credit Government will usher in the Leisure State gradually and smoothly, giving people time to readjust and re-educate themselves. And the rising generation—those born into a Leisure State—will shed the last vestiges of the 'fear of leisure', and live a life of intense activity and awareness such as their parents never knew. That is because they will have time to live, and to live splendidly.

56. *If We Are to Help the Poor, Isn't It Necessary to 'Soak the Rich'?*

No. That is like a man amputating his feet to cure his corns.

Not less for some, but more for all, is the right line of approach in a community that can produce enough and to spare for all its citizens.

59. *Wouldn't 'Common Ownership' Solve the Problem?*

No, it would not, because the problem has nothing to do with the ownership of anything. It is a problem of consumer markets—i.e., the buying power of money in your pocket, and mine.

Ownership does not give control over markets. If you and I, and everyone else, owned everything, everywhere, it would not, of itself, add one penny to our buying power.

For example, it is of no advantage to be able to say 'I, and 40,000,000 other people, own the railways'. The only question that matters is, 'Have I the money to buy a ticket so that I can use the railways?'

Ownership and Use are two quite different things, and what people want in a modern community is not to own things, but to be able to use them. Social Credit empowers them to do so by means of the National Dividend and Price Adjustment.

Ezra Pound

Ezra Pound

Ezra Pound, 1885–1972, described by *Who's Who in America*, as 'a principal founder and moving spirit of modern poetry in English', was also a dedicated opponent of the international bankers, and spent eleven years, undiagnosed, in St. Elizabeths mental asylum in Washington. While still at university Pound had started his magnum opus, *The Cantos*. In 1908 he travelled to Venice, where he paid for the printing of his first volume of poetry, *A Lume Spento*. He then went to London to meet W. B. Yeats and became a dominant figure in Yeats' literary circle, serving for a time as Yeats' secretary. He quickly gained recognition in London with the publication in 1909 of his poem '*Personae*'.

Pound came into contact with *The English Review*, which was publishing the works of D. H. Lawrence, and in 1911, with *The New Age* edited by the guild-socialist A. R. Orage, Pound himself launching the careers of William Carlos Williams, T. S. Eliot, Ernest Hemingway, and James Joyce. Orage's journal was both cultural and political. Orage propounded the revival of guilds as an alternative to the crass materialism of both capitalism and Marxism.

Like many of his friends such as Yeats, Wyndham Lewis, Eliot, et al Pound saw democracy as being the manipulation of the masses behind which stood the bankers. The money-rooted society was reducing the arts to profit-driven commodities.

Social Credit

Pound embraced the Social Credit theory of Major C. H. Douglas, whom he met in 1917 through Orage, who was promoting Douglas' ideas in *The English Review* and *The New Age*. T. S. Eliot expressed the outlook of many of those around Orage in his own journal, *The Criterion*, in January 1935: 'any real change for the better meant a spiritual revolution [and] that no spiritual revolution was of any use unless you had a practical economic system'.

Ezra Pound

Orage found in Douglas' theories the means of replacing the debt money system without which nothing else could be achieved. Such was Orage's influence that he even coined the term ' Social Credit', according to Social Crediters Frances Hutchinson and Brian Burkitt ('Major Douglas' Proposals for a National Dividend', *International Journal of Social Economics*, 21, 1994).

During the 1930s and 1940s Pound wrote a series of booklets on economics, 'Money Pamphlets by £', lucidly describing economic theory and history. Pound considered Fascist Italy to be partially achieving Social Credit aims in breaking the power of the bankers over politics and culture, writing: 'This will not content the Douglasites nor do I believe that Douglas' credit proposals can permanently be refused or refuted, but given the possibilities of intelligence against prejudice in the year XI of the Fascist Era, what other government has got any further, or shows any corresponding interest in or care for the workers?'(Pound, *Jefferson and/or Mussolini*, [1935] New York: Liveright, 1970, 126).

Pound and his wife Dorothy settled in Italy in 1924. He met Mussolini in 1933. He also became a regular contributor to the periodicals of Sir Oswald Mosley's British Union of Fascists, first writing to Mosley in 1934 and meeting him in 1936.

Writing in Mosley's *BUF Quarterly* in 1938, Pound stated that President Franklin D. Roosevelt and his New Deal 'brains trust' had betrayed the American Revolution. It was a theme he returned to in more detail during the war. Pound pointed out that Mussolini had instituted banking reform in 1935 and deplored the lack of knowledge and understanding around the world of what Italy was achieving. The U.S. Constitution gave the government the prerogative to create and issue its own credit and currency. Pound saw parallels between Fascist Italy and the type of economic system sought by certain American statesmen such as Jefferson and Andrew Jackson. The war was being fought in the interests of usury. These are the themes developed in Pound's series of pamphlets, and in his radio broadcasts from Rome.

In the British Union of Fascists, Pound found a congenial home for his economic theories. While the policy of 'state credit' advocated by fascists, was not the same as orthodox Social Credit, opposition to usury was a prime element of Mosley's British Fascism which, reminiscent of New Zealand's John A. Lee, had actually developed from Mosley's radical economic proposals while a rising star in the

British Labour Party, without recourse to foreign models. The British Union of Fascists director of policy, Alexander Raven Thomson, a widely educated economist, explained that a 'Fascist Government would issue the new currency and credit direct, without charge of usury...' (Thomson, *The Economics of British Fascism*, ca. 1935). Contrary to Douglas' Social Credit, Fascism contended that only a strong state could break the rule of the usurers. Thomson pointed out that merely 'nationalizing' the Bank of England would be of little use, as the bank would still be part of the international financial system. (This is something that John A. Lee was to point out in New Zealand, and Hargrave, as explained previously). Therefore a Fascist government would bring the 'control of currency out of the hands of the financial tyrants,' basing credit issue on the needs of production and consumption. (Thomson, *Our Financial Masters*, 1937).

Caged

In April 1939 Pound returned to the USA to garner support against America's entry into a war that he saw approaching against Germany. Opposition to the USA's entry into a war in Europe was running at 80% according to opinion polls, despite the war hysteria and Germanophobia being kicked up in the press, and by certain business and political interests. Movements such as America First, led by the charismatic aviation hero Charles Lindbergh, with support among Congressmen, Senators, and other prominent figures, were burgeoning. This caused much frustration for President Roosevelt and his backers, whose heralded 'New Deal' had been a failure, while Germany and Italy prospered under their new banking and trade systems.

In 1940, after having returned to Italy, Pound offered his services as a radio broadcaster. The broadcasts, called 'The American Hour', began in January 1941. In July 1943 Mussolini was deposed. Pound was indicted for treason by a grand jury in the District of Columbia, along with seven Americans who had been broadcasting for Germany. Ernest Hemingway, concerned at the fate of his old mentor, suggested the possibility of an 'insanity' plea. The idea caught on among some of Pound's literary friends who had obtained good jobs in the U.S. government during the war, while other interests were pressing for the death penalty. With the American invasion, Pound headed for the Salò Republic, the Fascist redoubt, where he wrote a flow of articles, mostly on economic reform, and in December, 1943 he resumed his radio broadcasts.

Ezra Pound

Mussolini was murdered on 28 April, 1945. On 2 May, Pound was taken from his home by Italian partisans after he had unsuccessfully attempted to turn himself over to the American forces. Putting a book on Confucius into his pocket, he went with the partisans expecting to be hanged, as a bloodlust was now turned against those who remained loyal to Mussolini. Instead, he ended up in an American camp at Pisa, constructed for the most vicious American military prisoners. Pound was confined in a bare iron cage in the burning heat, sleeping on the concrete floor, brilliantly lighted throughout the night. This was what Pound later called the 'gorilla cage'. *Esquire* commented: 'The dust and the light soon became intolerable; he became physically very weak; he lost his memory, eventually he broke down'. (Peter Ackroyd, *Ezra Pound and His World*, London, 86). He was transferred to a medical facility and lived in a small tent. 'Despite his extraordinary predicament, Pound's native spirit soon returned and he was writing his new Cantos'. (Ibid., 86).

In November 1945, he was flown to Washington and jailed. While Hemingway, et al. had planned to have Pound declared 'insane' to avoid treason charges, the conditions he had been subjected to had in fact caused him to mentally and physically break down. On 21 December he was sent to St. Elizabeths mental hospital. In February 1946 formal hearings declared him to be of unsound mind. He was kept at St. Elizabeths for eleven years, but conditions were rather good through the efforts of the friendly Superintendent, Dr Winfred Overholser. Here Pound's literary output continued. He translated 300 traditional Chinese poems that were published by Harvard University Press in 1954. He was awarded the Bollingen Prize for Poetry in 1949 for the '*Pisan Cantos*'. The award caused an uproar amidst accusations of 'Fascist infiltrators', but scholarly interest in Pound grew.

In 1958 the indictment for treason was dropped. On 30 June, 1958, Pound set sail for Italy. When he reached Naples, he gave the Fascist salute to journalists and declared, 'all America is an insane asylum'. He continued with '*The Cantos*', stayed in contact with political personalities such as Mosley, and remained defiantly opposed to the American system when giving interviews, despite the protests of U.S. diplomats to the Italian government.

In 1951, Peter Russell, a London publisher, reprinted many of Pound's pamphlets on economics, which he stated were 'essential to the full understanding of [Pound's] major poetical work, '*The Cantos*'. Russell commented that although the publication of the pamphlets had no political motive, they are 'a healthy reaction... to the vicious plutocracy and the destructive bureaucracy, which seem today to be the twin tyrants of our uneasy world'.

What is Money For?

We will never see an end of ructions, we will never have a sane and steady administration until we gain an absolutely clear conception of money. I mean an absolutely not an approximately clear conception.

I can, if you like, go back to paper money issued in China in or about A.D. 840, but we are concerned with the vagaries of the Western World. FIRST, Paterson, the founder of the Bank of England, told his shareholders that they would profit because "the bank hath profit on the interest of all the moneys which it creates out of nothing." What then is this "money" the banker can create out of nothing"?

Let us be quite clear. Money is a measured title or claim. That is its basic difference from unmeasured claims, such as a man's right to take all you've got under war-time requisition, or as an invader or thief just taking it all. Money is a measure which the taker hands over when be acquires the goods he takes. And no further formality need occur during the transfer, though sometimes a receipt is given. The idea of justice inheres in ideas of measure, and money is a measure of value.

Means Of Exchange

Money is valid when people recognise it as a claim and hand over goods or do work up to the value printed on the face of the ticket, whether it is made of metal or paper. Money is a general sort of ticket which is its only difference from a railway or theatre ticket. If this statement seems childish let the reader think for a moment about different kinds of tickets.

A railway ticket is a measured ticket. A ticket from London to Brighton differs from one for London to Edinburgh. Both are measured, but in miles that always stay the same length. A money ticket, under a corrupt system, wobbles. For a long time the public has trusted people whose measure was shifty.

Another angle. Theatre tickets are timed. You would probably not accept a ticket for Row H, Seat 27, if it were not dated. When six people are entitled to the same seat at the same time the tickets are not particularly good. (Orage asked; Would you call it inflation to print tickets for every seat in the house?) You will hear money called "a medium of exchange," which means that it can circulate freely, as a measure of goods and services against one another, from hand to hand.

Guarantee Of Future Exchange

We will have defined money properly when we have stated what it is in words that cannot be applied to anything else and when there is nothing about the essential nature of money that is omitted from our definition. When Aristotle calls money "a guarantee of future exchange" that merely means that it is an undated ticket, that will be good when we want to use it. Tickets have sometimes stayed good for a century. When we do not hand over money at once for goods or services received we are said to have "credit". The "credit" is the other man's belief that we can and will some time hand over the money or something measured by money.

Most men have been so intent on the individual piece of money, as a measure, that they have forgotten its purpose, and they have got into inextricable muddles and confusions regarding the total amount of money in a country. A perfectly good hammer is useless to pick your teeth with. If you don't know what money is FOR, you will get into a muddle when using it, and still more will a government get into a mess in its "monetary policy".

Statally speaking, that is from the point of view of a man or party that wants to govern justly, a piece of money is a ticket, the country's money is a mass of tickets for getting the country's food and goods justly distributed. The job for a man today who is trying to write a pamphlet on money is not to say something new, it is not to think up something or prove a theory, it is SIMPLY to make a clear statement about things that have been known for 200, and often for 2,000 years. You have got to know what money is FOR.

Purpose Of Money

If you think it is a mantrap or a means of bleeding the public, you will admire the banking system as run by the Rothschilds and international bankers. If you think it is a means of sweating profits out of the public, you will admire the stock exchange. Hence ultimately for the sake of keeping your ideas in order you will need a few principles.

Opposing the Money Lenders

THE AIM of a sane and decent economic system is to fix things so that decent people can eat, have clothes and houses up to the limit of available goods.

The Value Of Money

Take money in such a system as a means of exchange, and then realise that to be a just means of exchange it must be measured. What are you going to use to measure the value of anything? An egg is an egg. You can eat it (until it goes bad). Eggs are not all the same size, but they might serve among primitive people as an approximate measure.

Unterguggenberger, the Austrian monetary reformer, used WORK as a measure, "Arbeitswert," 10 schillings' worth of work. That was O.K. in a mountain valley where everyone could do pretty much the same kind of work in the fields. Charlemagne had a grain measure, so many pecks of barley, wheat or rye worth a DENAR, or put it the other way on. The just price of barley was so much the peck.

In 796 A.D. it was 2 denars. And in 808 A.D. it was 3 denars. That means that the farmer got more denars for the same quantity of barley. And let us hope he could buy more other goods with those denars. Unfortunately the worth of all things depends on whether there is a real scarcity, enough or more than can be used at a given time. A few eggs are worth a great deal to a hungry man on a raft. Wheat is worth MORE in terms of serge in some seasons than in others. So is gold, so is platinum. A single commodity (even gold) base for money is not satisfactory.

STATE AUTHORITY behind the printed note is the best means of establishing a JUST and HONEST currency. The Chinese grasped that over 1,000 years ago, as we can see from the Tang STATE (not Bank) NOTE. SOVEREIGNTY inheres in the right to ISSUE money (tickets) and to determine the value thereof.

American interests HIDE the most vital clause in our constitution. The American government hasn't, they say, the right to fix prices. BUT IT HAS THE RIGHT TO DETERMINE THE VALUE OF MONEY and this right is vested in Congress.

This is a mere difference in legal formalities and verbal arrangements. The U.S. Government has the right to say "a dollar is one wheat-bushel thick, it is one serge-foot long, it is ten gallons of petrol wide." Hence the U.S. Government could establish the JUST PRICE, and a just price system.

The Just Price

Out of barter grew the canonist doctrine of the just price, and a thousand years' thought from St. Ambrose to St. Antonino of Florence, as to HOW to determine the just price. Both the Douglas social crediters and modern Catholics POSTULATE the JUST PRICE as a necessary part of their Systems. The valid complaint against Douglas is that he didn't invent and set up machinery for ENFORCING the just price. A priest recently reported to me that the English distributists had about got round to realising that they had no mechanism for instituting and enforcing just price.

Only the STATE can effectively fix the JUST PRICE of any commodity by means of state-controlled pools of raw products and the restoration of guild organisation in industry.

The Quantity Of Money

Having determined the size of your dollar, or half-crown or shilling, your Government's next job is to see that TICKETS are properly printed and that they get to the right people.

The right people are all the people who've not engaged in CRIME, and crime for the duration of this pamphlet means among other things CHEATING the rest of the citizens through the money racket. In the United States and England there is NOT enough money. There are not enough tickets moving about among the WHOLE people to BUY what they need — EVEN when the goods are there on the counter or going to rot on the wharves.

When the total nation hasn't or cannot obtain enough food for its people, that nation is poor. When enough food exists and people cannot get it by honest labour, the state is rotten, and no effort of language will say how rotten it is. But for a banker or professor to tell you that the country cannot do this, that or the other because it lacks money is as black and foetid a lie, as grovelling and imbecile, as it would be to say it cannot build roads because it has no kilometres. (I didn't invent that phrase, but it is too good to leave idle.) Roosevelt and his professors were on the right line with their commodity dollar, BUT they hooeyed and smoke-screened and dodged the problem of having ENOUGH TICKETS to serve the whole people, and of keeping those tickets MOVING.

It is the business of the STATE to see that there is enough money in the hands of the WHOLE people, and in adequately rapid EXCHANGE, to effect distribution or all wealth produced and produceable. Until every member of the nation eats three times a day and has shelter and clothing, a nation is either lazy or unhealthy. If this occurs in a rich state the state's riches are not fully employed.

All value comes from labour. Wheat from ploughing, chestnuts from being picked up. BUT a lot of WORK has been done by men (mostly inventors, well-diggers, constructors of factory plant, etc.) now DEAD, and who therefore cannot eat and wear clothes.

Social Credit

In respect of this legacy of mechanical efficiency and scientific advance we have at our disposal a large volume of SOCIAL CREDIT, which can be distributed to the people as a bonus over and above their wage packet. Douglas proposed to bring up the TOTAL purchasing power of the whole people by a per capita issue of tickets PROPORTIONAL to available goods. In England and U.S. today available and desired goods remain unbought because the total purchasing power (i.e., total sum of tickets) is inadequate. Mussolini and Hitler wasted very little time PROPOSING. They started and DO distribute BOTH tickets and actual gopds on various graduated scales according to the virtues and activities of Italians and Germans. Douglas may object that this is not "democratic" (that is egalitarian) BUT for the monetary scientist or economist the result is the same. The goods are getting distributed.

There is a slightly different angle in the way these different men look on justice. They all agree that deficiency in a nation's total purchasing power must be made up. Ten or more years ago I said, that Mussolini had achieved more than Douglas, because Douglas has presented his ideas as a greed system, not as a will system.

Both Systems, Fascist and Douglasite, differ as the day from night from the degradation of the DOLE, from the infamy of the British system wherein men who are out of jobs are paid money taken from men who do work, and where the out-of-works are rendered progressively UNFIT to work or to enjoy the sensations of living. Not only are they a drag on workers, but they are made a drag on all people who are trying to maintain a decent standard of living. The whole scale of values is defiled. Every year sees less sense of SOCIAL VALUE; less sense of having people lead lives which do not harm others; of lives in which some measure and prudence is observed.

There is nothing new in creating money to distribute wealth. If you don't believe the Emperor Tching Tang issued the first national dividend in B.C. 1766 you can call it something else. It may have been an emergency dole, but the story will at least clear up one muddle. The emperor opened a copper mine and issued round coins with square holes and gave them to the poor "and this money enabled them to buy grain from the rich," but it had no effect on the general shortage of grain.

That story is 3,000 years old, but it helps one to understand what money is and what it can do. For the purpose of good government it is a ticket for the orderly distribution of WHAT IS AVAILABLE. It may even be an incentive to grow or fabricate more grain or goods, that is to attain abundance. But it is NOT in itself abundance.

Inflation

The term inflation is used as a bogey to scare people away from any expansion of money at all. Real INFLATION only begins when you issue MONEY (measured claims) against goods or services that are undeliverable (assignats of the French Revolution issued against state lands) or issue them in excess of those WANTED. That amounts to saying: two or more tickets for the same seat at the same time, or tickets in London for a theatre performance tonight in Bombay, or for a dud show.

Money can be expended as long as each measured claim can be honoured by the producers and distributors of the nation in the goods and services required by the public, when and where they want them. INFLATION is one danger; STAGNATION is another.

Gessel's Stamp Scrip

[Silvio] Gesell, the South American monetary reformer, saw the danger of money being hoarded and proposed to deal with it by the issue of "stamp scrip." This should be a government note requiring the bearer to affix a stamp worth up to 1% of its face value on the first day of every month. Unless the note carries its proper complement or monthly stamps it is not valid.

Opposing the Money Lenders

This is a form of TAX on money and in the case of British currency might take the form of 1/2d or 1d per month on a ten shilling note and 1d or 2d on a pound. There are any number of possible taxes, but Gesell's kind of tax can only fall on a man who has, in his pocket, at the moment the tax falls due, 100-times, at least, the amount of the tax.

Gesell's kind of money provides a medium and measure of exchange which cannot be hoarded with impunity. It will always keep moving. Bankers could NOT lock it up in their cellars and charge the public for letting it out. It has also the additional benefit of placing sellers of perishable goods at less of a disadvantage in negotiating with owners of theoretically imperishable money. I am particularly keen on Gesell, because once people have used stamp scrip they HAVE a clear idea about money, they understand tickets better than men who haven't used stamp scrip. I am no more anxious than anyone else to use a new kind of stamp, but I maintain that the public is NOT too stupid to use postage stamps and that there is no gain in pretending that they are too stupid to understand money.

I don't say you have to use Gesell's method. But once you understand WHY he wanted it you will not be fleeced by bank sharks and "monetary authorities" WITHOUT KNOWING HOW you are being fleeced. That is WHY Gesell is so useful as a school teacher. He proposed a very simple way of keeping his tickets moving.

Statal Money

In 1816 Thomas Jefferson made a basic statement that has NOT been properly digested, let alone brought into perspective with various "modern proposals" for special improvements of the present damned and destructive "system" or money racket. The reader had better FRAME Jefferson's statement:-

"And if the national bills issued be bottomed (as is indispensable) on pledges of specific taxes for their redemption within certain and moderate epochs, and be of proper denominations for circulation, no interest on them would be necessary or just, because they would answer to every one of the purposes of metallic money withdrawn and replaced by them." Jefferson to Crawford, 1816.

Jefferson's formula is SOLID. If the state emits ENOUGH money for valid and justifiable expenses and keeps it moving, circulating, going out the front door and coming in at the tax window, the nation will not suffer stagnation. The issue of HONEST MONEY is a service and when the state performs this service the state has a right to a just recompense, which differs from nearly all known forms of tax.

I say "when the state issues it," because when states are weak or incompetent or their issue inadequate, individuals and congeries of men or localities HAVE quite properly taken over this activity (or have retained it from pre-statal eras), and it is better, it is in fact necessary, that the function of the measure of exchange should be carried on than that it stop or break down altogether.

On the other hand a nation whose measure of exchange is at the mercy of forces OUTSIDE the nation, is a nation in peril, it is a nation without national sovereignty. It is a nation of incompetent idiots drifting to ruin. Let us repeat. Sovereignty inheres in the right to ISSUE measured claims to wealth, that is MONEY.

Necessary Safeguards

No part or function of government should be under closer surveillance, and in no part or cranny of government should higher moral criteria be ASSURED. STATAL MONEY based upon national wealth must replace GOLD manipulated by international usurers. The sane order in founding a dynasty or reorganising a government is:-

FIRST to get the results, that is to see that the people are fed and housed. THEN so to regulate the mechanism of distribution (monetary system or whatever) that it will not fall into decay and be pilfered.

For example J. Q. Adams, one of the American founders, had some nice socialist or statal ideas about reserving the national wealth for educational and "higher purposes". His proposals were UNTIMELY. Jackson opened the land; settlers could go and take quite a bit each, free and gratis. It was timely and useful. BUT no provision was made to prevent the settlers transferring this land WHEN THEY HAD NO FURTHER USE FOR IT and didn't want to work it themselves. Hence the U.S. land has fallen into great ownership. The same danger applies to monetary systems as to land settlement. Set up a perfect and just money system and in three days rascals, the bastards with mercantilist and monopolist mentality, will start thinking up some wheeze to cheat the people. The concessions-hunter will sprout in some new form as long as dung stinks and humanity produces mental abortions. John Adams early saw that stockjobbers would replace fat country small squire tyrants.

In the 1860s one of the Rothschilds was kind enough to admit that the banking system was contrary to public interest, and that was before the shadow of Hitler's jails had fallen ACROSS the family fortunes. It is this generation's job to do what was left undone by the early democrats. The guild system, endowing the people by occupation and vocation with corporate powers, gives them the means to protect themselves for all time from the money power.

If you don't like the guild idea, go get results with some other, but don't lose your head and forget what clean men are driving at. And don't lie to yourselves and mistake a plough for a mortgage and vice versa. It is useless to talk of economics or to listen to talk about economics or to read books on the subject until both reader and writer know what they mean by the half-dozen simplest and most necessary terms most frequently used.

An Economic System

The first thing for a man to think of when proposing an economic system is; WHAT IS IT FOR? And the answer is: to make sure that the whole people shall be able to eat (in a healthy manner), to be housed (decently) and be clothed (in a way adequate to the climate). Another form of that statement is Mussolini's:-

Discipline The Economic Forces And Equate Them To The Needs Of The Nation

The Left claim that private ownership has destroyed this true purpose of an economic system. Let us see how OWNERSHIP was defined, at the beginning of a capitalist era during the French Revolution.

> "OWNERSHIP is the right which every citizen has to enjoy and dispose of the portion of goods guaranteed him by the law. "The right of ownership is limited, as are all other rights by the obligation to respect the rights of others. It cannot be prejudicial to the safety, nor to the liberty nor to the existence, nor to the ownership of other men like ourselves Every possession, every traffic, which violates this principle is illicit and immoral." – Robespierre.

Ezra Pound

USURY

The perspective of the damned XIXth century shows little else than the violation of these principles by demoliberal usuriocracy. The doctrine of Capital, in short, has shown itself as little else than the idea that unprincipled thieves and antisocial groups should be allowed to gnaw into the rights of ownership. This tendency "to gnaw into" has been recognised and stigmatised from the time of the laws of Moses and he called it neschek. And nothing differs more from this gnawing or corrosive than the right to share out the fruits of a common co-operative labour.

Indeed USURY has become the dominant force in the modern world. "Moreover, imperialism is an immense accumulation of money capital in a few countries, which, as we have seen, amounts to 4 or 5 thousand million pounds sterling in securities. Hence the extraordinary growth of a class, or rather a Stratum, of rentiers, i.e, persons who live by "clipping coupons" who take absolutely no part in any enterprise, and whose profession is idleness. The exportation of capital, one of the most essential economic bases of imperialism, still further isolates this rentier stratum from production, and sets the seal of parasitism on the whole country living on the exploitation of the labour of several overseas countries and colonies." V. I. Lenin, quoting Hobson in "Imperialism, the highest stage of Capitalism."

Very well! That is from Lenin. But you could quote the same substance from Hitler, who is a Nazi (note the paragraph from *"Mein Kampf"* magnificently isolated by Wyndham Lewis in his *"Hitler"* – "The struggle against international finance and loan capital has become the most important point in the National Socialist programme; the struggle of the German nation for its independence and freedom."

You could quote it from Mussolini, a Fascist, or from C. H. Douglas, who calls himself a democrat and his followers the only true democrats. You could quote it from McNair Wilson who is a Christian Monarchy man. You could quote it from a dozen camps which have no suspicion they are quoting Lenin. The only people who do not seem to have read and digested this essay of his are the British Labour Party and various groups of professing communists throughout the Occident.

Some facts are now known above parties, some perceptions are the common heritage of all men of good will and only the Jewspapers and worse than Jewspapers, try now to obscure them. Among the worse

Opposing the Money Lenders

than Jewspapers we must list the hired professors who misteach new generations of young, who lie for hire and who continue to lie from sheer sloth and inertia and from dog-like contempt for the wellbeing of all mankind. At this point, and to prevent the dragging of red herrings, I wish to distinguish between prejudice against the Jew as such and the suggestion that the Jew should face his own problem.

Does he in his individual case wish to observe the law of Moses? Does he propose to continue to rob other men by usury mechanism while wishing to be considered a "neighbour"? This is the sort or double-standard which a befouled English delegation tried to enforce via the corrupt League of Nations (frontage and face wash for the worse international corruption at Basel).

USURY is the cancer of the world, which only the surgeon's knife of Fascism can cut out of the life of the nations.

Ezra Pound – 1935

Father Charles Coughlin

Father Charles Coughlin

For centuries, as we have seen in the "Introduction," the Catholic Church had condemned usury as a sin, and money-lenders charging interest on loans were regarded as among the lowest of people frequently subjected to riots and even death. The Church also developed a social doctrine that culminated in the Encyclical of Pope Leo XIII, *Rerum Novarum* (1891) in regard to the relations of Labour and Capital, as an alternative to what the Church saw as the twin atheistic materialism of socialism and capitalism. In 1931 Pius XI issued his Encyclical letter *Quadragesimo Anno*. Both capitalism and socialism concentrated property rather than allowing its ownership widely; capitalism by placing ownership in the hands of a few private owners; socialism by concentrating property in the hands of the state.

This social doctrine inspired significant movements, including in England the *Distributist* movement headed by the well-known Catholic authors Hilaire Belloc and G. K. Chesterton, and many Catholics supported Social Credit. In the USA the world-wide reaction against rapacious capitalism and its rulers, the international bankers, took its most significant form in Father Charles Coughlin's National Union for Social Justice.

In Canada in 1939 another remarkable Catholic movement dedicated to Church social doctrine, with the focus on Social Credit, was the Pilgrims of St. Michael, established by Louis Even and Gilberte Côté-Mercier. Also known as the White Berets the movement still exists and has maintained its crusading zeal, publishing its journal *Michael*, since 1939 and increasing the editions from French, to English, Polish and Spanish. The movement explains that in accord with the Church's historical teachings against usury,

> "Louis Even decided to spread the Social Credit doctrine — a set of principles and financial proposals conceived in 1917 by the Scottish engineer, Clifford Hugh Douglas, to solve the problem of poverty and of the chronic shortage of purchasing power in the hands of the consumers. The words 'social credit' means social

money, or national money, money issued by society, as opposed to the present money that is a 'banking credit', money issued by the banks. The Catholic Church teaches principles of social justice (known as 'the social doctrine of the Church'), but leaves to the faithful the task of finding concrete ways of implementing these principles. To our knowledge, the Social Credit principles are one of the best ways to apply these principles of justice in economics."

Among the books that the Pilgrims recommend is Canadian-born Father Coughlin's book *Money—Questions and Answers*.

Radio Priest

Charles Edward Coughlin was born in Hamilton, Ontario, 25 October, 1891. From his teen years he knew his vocation was to be a priest. He was ordained to the priesthood in 1916. He taught for seven years at the Assumption College in Ontario, and moved to Detroit in 1923. He started a church in Royal Oak, Michigan, with a congregation of 28 families. He called it the Shrine of the Little Flower Church. A baseball fan, he met Dick Richards owner of the Detroit Tigers, who offered to sponsor a half hour talk on his radio station. Father Coughlin began his Sunday radio broadcasts on WJR in 1926. The themes were the family, with emphasis on speaking to children. One anti-Coughlin critic, Wallace Stegner, recalled that in the midst of despair Father Coughlin's voice was 'of such mellow richness, such manly, heart-warming, confidential intimacy, such emotional and ingratiating charm, that anyone tuning past it almost automatically returned to hear it again. It was without doubt one of the great speaking voices of the twentieth century'. ('The Radio Priest and His Flock', *The Aspirin Age*, London, 1950).

The popularity was quick and donations flowed in to purchase time on other stations. The show was picked up by CBS. His congregation increased to 2,600 families, and a 180 foot tower was added to the Church which was used for broadcasting.

On 30 January 1930 Father Coughlin broadcast his first political talk, referring to 'the Bolsheviks and the bankers who support them'. He attacked President Herbert Hoover. Senator Hamilton Fish Jr., asked Coughlin to testify in Washington about Communism. His broadcasts were suddenly dropped by CBS in 1931. However, Coughlin appealed to his listeners for funds and with mail reaching 80,000 letters a week, he soon developed his own radio network reaching an estimated ten million listeners. (Stegner, ibid.). In Royal Oak a new post office was built just to handle the amount of mail Coughlin was receiving.

During the 1932 Presidential election Coughlin avidly promoted the candidacy of Franklin D. Roosevelt with the slogan 'Roosevelt or ruin', describing Roosevelt's plan of a 'New Deal' to get the American economy running again as 'Christ's Deal'. By this time the radio audience was estimated at 30,000,0000 to 45,000,000. Roosevelt met Coughlin several times to obtain his support, and Coughlin wrote several of Roosevelt's speeches. The Catholic hierarchy approved, and Pope Pius was said to have written to Coughlin congratulating him on his espousal of Catholic social doctrine.

Once Roosevelt had assumed the Presidency, Coughlin soon saw him as a puppet of the international bankers. The break with Roosevelt became public in March 1933 with Coughlin broadcasting that Roosevelt now considered him a "burden."

Social Justice

In late 1934 Father Coughlin established the National Union for Social Justice, to campaign against the money-changers. Announcing his platform in November 1934, he referred to the Great War as having delivered "Waste and destruction of property, the desolation of homes and farms, the decay of factories and industries... They were years when innocent civilians of all countries were bowed down by the regimented forces of greed, of selfishness, of crass ignorance and of obstinacy." He referred to the New Deal as "on trial" and hoped that it would succeed. If the flaws of capitalism and industrialism were not eliminated Communism would result. Suggesting a social credit type "National Dividend," or what is today often called a "guaranteed basic income," Coughlin said that there must be a just annual wage for all citizens. Of World War I: 'we are convinced that it was one organized and operated for commercial purposes and commercial gains. Every cannon forged, every shell exploded was trade-marked with the sign of decadent capitalism. It was a war fought to make the world safe for Wall Street and for the international bankers'. The war had changed economic necessities.

> "First: Unemployment on a huge scale was an absolute certainty, if we still held to the proposition that a laborer should be paid 50 cents an hour while he worked and then be left to seek refuge in

a dole line until the motor cars, the locomotives, the shoes and other products of a factory were being consumed.

"Second: The theory that production for a profit existed for industrialists and stockholders only, and not for laborers and mechanics, was no longer tenable. If laborers were required to work only six or eight months in the year under a wage scale that paid them while they worked and starved them while they were idle, then a new annual wage scale must be adopted.

"This, then, was no depression. It simply marked the end of an era where man's problem was formerly one of production. It announced the birth of a new era where henceforth our problem shall be one of distribution of the profits not only to the owners and stockholders but also to the laborers and mechanics, enabling all to live prosperously even when the wheels of industry have ceased operating."

The problem of the era was one of distribution:

"Now, my friends, let no one deceive you with the economic lie that there is over-production when millions are hungry, when millions more are in the bread line and when 16 million homes in America are deprived of the ordinary conveniences of life—running water, modern plumbing, electricity and modern heat.

"There is simply a lack of distribution.

"Distribution of wealth is substantially associated with the problem of money—with the problem of 50 cents an hour while you work and the soup line while you are idle; with the problem of a destroyed purchasing power; with the problem of organized doles and disorganized taxation; with the problem of impending communism.

"If there is plenty for all in this country—plenty of fields of wheat and of cotton, plenty of factories, mechanics and scientists—the only reason why this plenitude of God's blessing is not shared by all is because our Government has not, as yet, faced the problem of distribution. In other words, it may boast that it has driven the money changers from the temple but it permits industry to cling tenaciously to the cast-off philosophy of the money changers. Our Government still upholds one of the worst evils of decadent capitalism, namely, that production must be only at a profit for the owners, for the capitalist, and not for the laborer. This philosophy of finance, or of distribution of profits, based on the theory of 'pay-while-you-work' for the laborer can only be identified with destruction of the entire system of capitalism."

What Coughlin was advocating was in accord with the social doctrine of the Church and Pope Leo's *Rerum Novarum*: that capital and labour are symbiotic, ownership has a social function, and owners have a social duty:

> "Are those of you who own and control wealth ignorant of the fact that labor owes no rights to capital unless capital performs its duty towards labor? Are you forgetful, ye princes of this world's goods, that you are no better than stewards designated to manage justly and fairly the property of this world which belongs not to you but to the God who created you?
>
> "My friends, the outworn creed of capitalism is done for. The clarion call of communism has been sounded. They are both rotten! But it is not necessary to suffer any longer the slings and arrows of modern capitalism any more than it is to surrender our rights to life, to liberty and to the cherished bonds of family to communism.
>
> "The high priests of capitalism bid us beware of the radical and call upon us to expel him from our midst. There will be no expulsion of radicals until the causes which breed radicals will first be destroyed! The apostles of Lenin and Trotsky bid us forsake all rights to private ownership and ask us to surrender our liberty for that mess of pottage labeled 'prosperity,' while it summons us to worship at the altar where a dictator of flesh and blood is enthroned as our god and the citizens are branded as his slaves. Away with both of them! But never into the discard with the liberties which we have already won and the economic liberty which we are about to win or die in the attempt!"

Coughlin announced the formation of the National Union for Social Justice to lobby for this. However, it was not confined to a religious denomination, age, class, or race.

> "How shall we organize? To what principles of social justice shall we pledge ourselves ? What action shall we take? These are

Father Charles Coughlin

practical questions which I ask myself as I recognize the fact that this NATIONAL UNION FOR SOCIAL JUSTICE must be established in every county and city and town in these United States of America. It is for the youth of the nation. It is for the brains of the nation. It is for the farmers of the nation. It is for everyone in the nation."

Coughlin announced the sixteen principles for the NUSJ:

1. I believe in liberty of conscience and liberty of education, not permitting the state to dictate either my worship to my God or my chosen avocation in life.

2. I believe that every citizen willing to work and capable of working shall receive a just, living, annual wage which will enable him both to maintain and educate his family according to the standards of American decency.

3. I believe in nationalizing those public resources which by their very nature are too important to be held in the control of private individuals.

4. I believe in private ownership of all other property.

5. I believe in upholding the right to private property but in controlling it for the public good.

6. I believe in the abolition of the privately owned Federal Reserve Banking system and in the establishment of a Government owned Central Bank.

7. I believe in rescuing from the hands of private owners the right to coin and regulate the value of money, which right must be restored to Congress where it belongs.

8. I believe that one of the chief duties of this Government owned Central Bank is to maintain the cost of living on an even keel and arrange for the repayment of dollar debts with equal value dollars.

9. I believe in the cost of production plus a fair profit for the farmer.

10. I believe not only in the right of the laboring man to organize in unions but also in the duty of the Government, which that

Opposing the Money Lenders

laboring man supports, to protect these organizations against the vested interests of wealth and of intellect.

11. I believe in the recall of all non-productive bonds and therefore in the alleviation of taxation.

12. I believe in the abolition of tax-exempt bonds.

13. I believe in broadening the base of taxation according to the principles of ownership and the capacity to pay.

14. I believe in the simplification of government and the further lifting of crushing taxation from the slender revenues of the laboring class.

15. I believe that, in the event of a war for the defense of our nation and its liberties, there shall be a conscription of wealth as well as a conscription of men.

16. I believe in preferring the sanctity of human rights to the sanctity of property rights; for the chief concern of government shall be for the poor because, as it is witnessed, the rich have ample means of their own to care for themselves.

"These are my beliefs. These are the fundamentals of the organization which I present to you under the name of the NATIONAL UNION FOR SOCIAL JUSTICE. It is your privilege to reject or to accept my beliefs; to follow me or to repudiate me.

"Hitherto you have been merely an audience. Today, in accepting the challenge of your letters, I call upon everyone of you who is weary of drinking the bitter vinegar of sordid capitalism and upon everyone who is fearsome of being nailed to the cross of communism to join this Union which, if it is to succeed, must rise above the concept of an audience and become a living, vibrant, united, active organization, superior to politics and politicians in principle, and independent of them in power.

"...It shall be a Union for the employed and the unemployed, for the old and the young, for the rich and the poor, independent of race, color or creed. It is my answer to the challenge received from the youth of the nation; my answer to those who have dared me to act!

Father Charles Coughlin

"This is the new call to arms—not to become cannon fodder for the greedy system of an outworn capitalism nor factory fodder for the slave whip of communism. This is the new call to arms for the establishment of social justice! God wills it! Do you?"

Coughlin backed former Governor of Louisiana, Senator Huey Long, whose "Share the Wealth" movement, with its slogan "every man a king," challenged Roosevelt and the oligarchs. "Share the Wealth" became a mass movement across the USA, led by an aide of Long, Gerald L. K. Smith. When Long, who could well have become President, was assassinated in 1936, Smith attempted to hold the Long movement together. Coughlin, Smith and Dr. Francis Townsend's large social pension movement, joined forces and formed the Union Party. William Lemke, Congressman for North Dakota, ran as its presidential candidate, but with poor results (2%). He was however re-elected to Congress. Although a Republican, Lemke had supported the New Deal and was known for his support for the farmer. He had tried to introduce legislation against the foreclosure of farmers. In 1934 Lemke co-sponsored a bill that would allow the Government to refinance farm mortgages, but it was scotched by Roosevelt.

In 1938, with *Social Justice* salesmen being attacked in the streets by Communists and Jews, the Christian Front was formed as a self-defence force. This attracted wild allegations from government and media that a militia was being formed, and "platoons" were subjected to FBI raids.

In mid 1940 many important radio networks refused to renew their contract for Coughlin's program, including NBC, CBS and Mutual Broadcasting, citing the 1939 National Association of Broadcasters rules, specifically drafted to stop Coughlin, that placed increased limitations on the sale of radio time to controversial spokesmen.

After Pearl Harbor, Coughlin continued to expose the war-mongers in Washington and elsewhere, the same forces that he had long shown had profited from World War I. In 1942, the FBI raided the Church of the Shrine of the Little Flower and seized all parish records and personal papers. Then, with distribution of his magazine *Social Justice* reaching 900,000 the Roosevelt administration removed Father Coughlin's mailing rights. The ban was overcome by utilising the NUSJ's grass roots network.

Opposing the Money Lenders

Other than assassination, like Huey Long, there was only one other way that Coughlin could be silenced. On 1 May, 1942, Archbishop Edward Mooney, the new head of the Detroit diocese, ordered Coughlin to stop all non-pastoral activities or face being defrocked. Gerald L. K. Smith, who was visiting Coughlin at his church on the day, related that Bishop Gallagher, who had supported Coughlin, came in with a Vatican prelate (presumably Mooney). Bishop Gallagher had a private conversation with Coughlin for a few minutes. Coughlin returned and told Smith:

> "The Pope has been wanting the President to appoint a Fraternal Delegate for diplomatic purposes, but no President has ever been willing to do it because of the strong pressure from Protestant [or Masonic?] organizations against it. But now, Mr. Roosevelt, who was burning under the pressure of my broadcasts, has served notice on the Pope that if he will silence me he will appoint a Fraternal Delegate to the Vatican. This means that I will never broadcast again except strictly religious comment." (Smith, *Besieged Patriot*, 1978, "Episode 35").

Coughlin continued his pastoral duties at his church until his retirement in 1966. He died in 1979; one of the Church's and the USA's most effective advocates of Catholic social doctrine. His policy could have succeeded where the much-hyped New Deal had failed, and the USA did not assume economic revival until World War II.

The following chapters are extracted from Father Coughlin's 1936 book *Money—Questions and Answers*. It is likely to be one of the most cogent expositions of banking reform in the English language, and shows something of Coughlin's straight-forward manner and efficacy as a teacher to millions.

Father Charles Coughlin

Money Questions and Answers

Dedicated To The Oppressed People Of America

Preface

This book is written for the ordinary American citizen. Therefore many needlessly abstract and intricate questions dealing with political economy, banking, and money are purposely omitted.

Unlike many writers on money, the author is in nowise identified with that band of political economists who have proven to be nothing more than mouthpieces for the private coiners of money.

Moreover, the author of this book has kept in mind the vast resources and virgin wealth of the United States of America where want needlessly reigns in the midst of plenty simply because there is a planned scarcity of money required for the transfer of wealth.

The National Union which is propagating the doctrine of social justice presents this book to the American public in order to expand principles number six, number seven and number eight of the sixteen principles of social justice which have been widely publicized. These specific principles are as follows:

6. I believe in the abolition of the privately owned Federal Reserve Banking System and in the establishment of a Government owned Central Bank.

7. I believe in rescuing from the hands of private owners the right to coin and regulate the value of money, which right must be restored to Congress where it belongs.

8. I believe that one of the chief duties of this Government owned Central Bank is to maintain the cost of living on an even keel and arrange for the repayment of dollar debts with equal value dollars.

In no sense, however, should this book be misinterpreted to mean that the National Union has discarded other principles. Because money is the most vital and fundamental problem to be solved before social justice can be reestablished, this is the first of a series of books which will deal with the entire program of social justice.

Opposing the Money Lenders

It is hoped that the possessor of this book will not content himself with merely reading, but will acquire a fluent knowledge of the truths herein contained to the end that he will be able to instruct his fellow citizens on the money question. Needless to remark, it is not convenient for the public press either to explain or to uphold many of the teachings herein contained. Consequently, it is believed that this book will be of service to the misinformed and uninformed public.

Someone suggested to me that the proper title for this book should be "Your Money or Your Life!" Such a title is rather suggestive of Jesse James and of John Dillinger. Upon second thought, the title was discarded, not because it did not cryptically express the real substance of this book, but, rather, because the pages of this volume are dedicated to an earnest, class-roomish exposition of simple economic truths which are intimately concerned with the nature of money.

While the title of the book should be conservative, I readily confess that unless we American citizens recapture our sovereign right of coining and regulating the value of our money and of foreign coin (not permitting this Congressional function to be exercised by a few privately licensed individuals for their own profit) it is apparent that it is "your money or your life." It will be only a matter of years before the liberties identified with our democracy must be bartered for the privilege of eking out an existence under a political system of some kind of tyranny if we continue using the privately created money of those who do not work or produce to obtain money and who can manipulate the volume in existence.

In truth, it is either your money or your democratic life. It is either your money or your American standard of life. It is either your money or the Christian concept of life.

Centuries ago, long before printing and engraving were invented, our European forefathers employed gold and silver, impressed with the stamp of the sovereign government, as their circulating medium. It was their custom to deposit their surplus coins with a man who was ingenious enough to construct a strong room inaccessible to thieves. In return, the strong room keeper gave the depositors a slip of paper best described as a receipt which, on presentation, enabled the depositor to take out his gold or silver on demand.

Many strong room keepers began doing business in the more populous centers of European countries. It was not long until they discovered

Father Charles Coughlin

that honest depositors (believing that the strong room keepers were as honest as themselves) did not call regularly for their gold, but preferred to transfer among themselves the slips of paper or the receipts. At least 90% of the gold and silver depositors adopted this practice.

Thus it was, taking advantage of this practice, that the strong room keepers began to issue more receipts for deposited gold than there was actual gold in their vaults. They practiced a confidence game. They commercialized upon the credulity of their depositors.

For example: Some enterprising merchant, anxious to invest in a foreign cargo, required immediate money to transact his business. A strong room keeper, knowing that his real depositors likely would not be demanding their gold, loaned this enterprising merchant a handful of receipts which were really promises-to-pay in gold. The truth of it was, the strong room keeper did not have that much gold in his vaults. I repeat, he was commercializing upon the credulity of his real depositors and, at the same time, was thereby actually lending money which did not exist. There was no government stamp upon his receipts or his promises-to-pay.

This, gentle reader, (it were better, perchance, were I to call you "indignant reader") was the origin of the bankers' racket which was actually legalized towards the end of the Seventeenth Century. In 1694 A.D., King William of England passed a law in the British House of Parliament legalizing this practice which commercialized the credulity of honest men, by permitting the privately owned Bank of England to become the legalized counterfeiters of English money.

Times have not changed, nor has the practice of the banking fraternity. The Jesse Jameses and the John Dillingers who went about with sawed-off shot guns relieving citizens either of their hard-earned wealth or of their receipts for it, have been outmoded and outstripped by those who, in the process of the evolution of brigandry, have put aside the black mask in favor of the white carnation and the shot gun in preference for a purple fountain pen.

Brigandry, legal or illegal, must cease. The credulity of a civilized people must give way to intelligence. Paying interest on money not originated by our government, but originated by private individuals, must terminate. It is either your money or your life.

With a knowledge of the answers given to the following questions contained within this book, you and I will be in a position to recapture our sovereign right and bring to an end the social immorality from which we are suffering.

Wealth

1. What is wealth?—Wealth consists of the things persons use to sustain and empower life or to produce the things which sustain life.

2. What are the common forms of wealth?—Food, clothing, shelter, etc.—all things necessary for living.

3. Are there various species of wealth?—Yes. There are material, intellectual and spiritual species of wealth.

4. Are we discussing all species of wealth?—No, only the material. However, be it remarked that social morality, intellectual good and spiritual sanctity are tremendously affected if material wealth is needlessly denied to citizens.

5. From what is this material wealth produced?—From the natural resources of creation.

6. Does man produce this wealth?—Only in a secondary sense. First, he must have the natural resources which he converts into forms convenient for human use.

7. What are the principal natural resources?—Lands, minerals, air, water, forest, sunlight and atomic energy.

8. Can wealth be created out of nothing?—No. It is a product of human activity expended upon the raw materials and the sources of everything in creation.

9. What is the purpose of all human activity and industry?—To produce and distribute an ever increasing volume of life-sustaining goods and services.

10. What are the two main classes of wealth produced?—The first class consists of the things which man directly consumes or uses up in living. These are called "consumer goods" or perishable goods used and consumed in actually sustaining life; e. g. food,

clothing, fuel, etc. The second class consists of capital or producer goods; e.g. a factory, freight car, or machine is wealth that is not consumed by human beings but helps to produce and distribute the things they consume in sustaining life.

11. Can wealth be consumed more than once?—No. Food, when eaten; clothing, when worn; or fuel, when burned has been used up and cannot be consumed again. What remains is waste matter.

12. Are producer goods wealth already consumed?—Yes, generally, in the sense that raw materials have been converted into specific pieces of machinery, buildings, etc. They are useful as things into which they were converted, but they cannot be reconverted into the original raw materials without the expenditure of more work.

13. Do producer goods wear out and grow obsolete?—Yes, and for that reason the owners of those producer goods should obtain a part of the new wealth produced, so long as those specific tools or implements of production are in efficient use.

14. What are the limitations to the production of consumer wealth at any given time?—The natural resources, the plants and machinery in usable condition, and the workers capable of directing and operating the necessary processes.

15. When producer goods wear out, what must be done?—They must be replaced by constructing new producer goods out of available consumer goods. The consumer goods do not become producer goods until they are fabricated into permanent form; e.g. iron ore into a machine, sand into a concrete building.

16. When producer goods are idle, do all citizens suffer an economic loss? (e.g. an idle shoe factory)—Yes, because these goods (the machinery) are not used to turn out the volume of consumer goods (shoes) for which they were built. When a smaller volume of consumer goods is produced, human beings have less of the necessities of life. The greatest loss is that of time passed in idleness, which can never be retrieved and of useless privation, which is destructive of well-being.

17. Are gold and silver consumer wealth?—Only in the very limited sense of being worn as jewelry, fillings for teeth, and for decorative purposes.

Opposing the Money Lenders

18. Has the United States produced too much wealth?—No. There are available volumes of authentic figures indicating that the production of all classes of wealth have been far short of the amount required to provide those willing and capable of working with the reasonable physical necessities to maintain a healthful life.

19. What percentage of our population is merely existing rather than enjoying the use of available and sufficient wealth to live in reasonable comfort?—At least three-fourths of our total population.

Recapitulation

1. To sustain life, material wealth is necessary.

2. Material wealth consists of consumer wealth and producer wealth.

3. (a) Consumer wealth is used up by once using.

   (b) Producer wealth, while not sustaining life directly, is used to produce consumer wealth.

4. Consumer wealth produced to satisfy every human need is the object of human, economic activity.

5. Human economic activity has not produced too much wealth.

Money

1. What is money?

A medium of exchange used as a reckoner or counter to avoid the direct exchange of goods for goods.

2. What is the function of money?

To make easy the exchange of goods and services, so that when one parts with anything having exchange value without needing anything in return immediately, he can keep the money until he does. It is an evidence that he has contributed some goods or services which society wants, and is a demand on that society for an equal value of what he may require at any time the need arises.

3. Then what may be used as money?

Money is anything commonly used and accepted as a medium of exchange. Money is the evidence that the possessor has parted with commodities or services and has not yet received its equivalent. Therefore, in the final analysis, money may be any object (paper, metal, beads) used as the receipt or acknowledgment of delivery of goods or services having exchange value, as long as it is recognized as such by its users and those by whose sovereign power it was created.

4. Does one who possesses money own wealth?

No. The possession of money is the evidence that the holder is owed wealth by the community.

5. Is one who holds money voluntarily abstaining from the ownership and use of wealth?

Yes, the owner of money is owed wealth. Money is accepted and held to suit the convenience of the possessor, so long as he knows that he can exchange it for wealth when he wants wealth.

6. Is the substance of which money is made important?

No. It is the legal status given it by government stamp that makes it acceptable by all as money, whether it be made of metal (punch press money), or of paper (printing press money).

"Money is a value created by law, to be a scale of valuation and a valid tender for payments." (Cernuschi, Italian Economist, in "Numisma or Legal Tender").

"An article is determined to be money by reason of the performance by it of certain functions, without regard to its form or substance;" (American Cyclopedia, Vol. II, Page 735).

"Money has value only by law and not by nature." (From "Politics" by Aristotle).

7. Of what importance is the seal or imprint upon money?

It is the public seal or stamp imprinted upon the substance that makes it money.

"The currency value is in the stamp, when used as money, and not in the use of the metal independent of the stamp. In other words, the money quality is the authority which makes it current and gives it power to accomplish the purpose for which it was created." (From *Government and Constitutional Law* by Judge Joel Tiffany, Page 221).

8. *Can either paper or metal be used to receive the public seal or imprint and thereby become money?*

Yes. With modern engraving processes that make imitation difficult, paper is more suitable than metal, because it is only the sovereign stamp or seal of the Government which can give it legal quality. All money is created under law.

9. *Why were metals, such as gold or silver, ever used for money?*

Because they were durable substances and could not be easily counterfeited, and because printing and engraving were not invented.

10. *What seal or imprint should always be placed upon money?*

That of the National Government.

The Attorney General of the United States, speaking of the Legal Tender Acts (12 Wallace, U.S. Supreme Court Reports, Page 319) says:

"This legislation assumes that, in contemplation of law, money of every species has the value which law fixes on it. . . . We repeat: Money is not a substance hut an impression of legal authority, a printed legal decree."

11. *Why should the seal of the National Government be the only seal or imprint allowed?*

Because it is the sovereign stamp or seal of the Government which gives it legal quality.

"The Constitution was intended to frame a government, supreme in some particulars, over States and people. It was designed to provide the same currency, having a uniform legal value in all states." (12 Wallace Reports, Knox vs. Lee, et. al. and Parker vs. Davis, Statement by Justice Strong of the United States Supreme Court).

12. Under existing laws (February 1936), does our National Government originate our money?

No, only to a very limited extent.

13. Who does originate (create) our money?

Private corporations, commonly called banks, now originate practically all of our money.

14. Why have private individuals usurped and exercised the sovereign power of issuing our money?

Because when that power is held and exercised by private individuals, they can and do control the entire economic, social and governmental system and derive enormous, illicit profits therefrom.

15. Why does the Constitution provide that the power to originate money should be confined to the National Congress?

Because the power to issue money and determine what volume shall be in use is the sovereign power. It is the greatest power inherent in any people who constitute a nation.

16. How do you get money?

You get money for work performed or services rendered in producing and distributing wealth.

17. What functions does money perform for you?

It bridges the time between the sale of your wealth or services, and the purchase of wealth as needed. It also enables you to exchange one thing for a number of things, or vice versa; it enables you to exchange your labor for a large number of articles, instead of forcing you to take, as your pay, a portion of your personal production. This ready divisibility of money into many small parts is one of the advantages of using money.

18. Where does this money originally come from?

Money is man-made. It comes from whoever exercises the power to originate or create it.

19. Since money is man-made, is this not a case of the originator

getting "something-for-nothing", which we are told is impossible?

Yes; and those who create our money under the present Federal Reserve Banking system, for the trivial cost of bookkeeping entries or engraving paper, create out of nothing the money which they lend to us at interest.

20. Do these Federal Reserve Bankers, who sneer at the idea of getting something-for-nothing, know that this is precisely what happens under our present illicit money-creating system?

Whether or not they do, the fact remains, that they use this very principle to accomplish the concentration of the ownership of wealth in the hands of a few and the impoverishment of the many. The success with which they have used this vicious principle indicates that their operations have not been haphazard, but deliberately and carefully planned.

21. Does their money, when it leaves the possession of the creators, buy wealth, just as your money buys wealth when you surrender it?

Yes, because after they create it, they lend it to others to buy wealth.

22. Who should create money?

The Government, representing all of the people.

23. In our country, what governing body should represent all of the people?

The Congress of the United States.

24. Who, then, should originate all of our money?

Congress.

25. How could the American people benefit by Congress alone originating money?

Each would receive his proportionate benefit from the original purchasing power, for the Government would pay money into use in return for public goods and services needed, and in performing the proper functions of government. e.g.: When $1,000 leaves the possession of the originator, it purchases $1,000 worth of wealth, just as the $1,000 you earned and saved will purchase an identical quantity of wealth when it leaves your possession.

26. Under our present private money-creating system, what do the bankers get for nothing?

They get interest on the money they create and lend, and title to people's properties by confiscation of properties pledged, if the loans are not repaid at a specific time.

27. Does the Constitution of the United States provide that Congress should originate our money?

Yes. It is very specific and well defined: "Congress shall have the power to coin money and regulate the value thereof, and of foreign coin". Article I, Section 8, Part 5.

"Whatever power there is over the currency is vested in Congress. If that power to declare what is money is not in Congress, it is annihilated." (Justice Strong of the United States Supreme Court, Knox vs. Lee, 12 Wallace Reports).

28. Why did the Framers of the Constitution place the power to coin money and regulate the value thereof in the Congress of the United States?

Because they understood the fundamental principles of government, and the blessings of an honest money system as against the curse of a dishonest one.

29. Can Congress delegate a power, reserved to it by the Constitution as a public function, to be operated for private profit without specifications?

No, not without violating the Constitution of the United States.

30. Has Congress delegated for private profit and without specification the power to originate our money?

Yes, by the National Bank Act of 1863 and the Federal Reserve Act of 1913, as well as intermediary and subsequent enactments.

31. But, are these not laws, passed by Congress?

No.! They are violations of Constitutional law, passed by Congress just as were the AAA (Agricultural Adjustment Administration) and NRA (National Recovery Act).

32. Why does this violation continue?

Opposing the Money Lenders

Because every time a Franklin, a Jefferson, a Jackson, or a Lincoln, or any other honest public servant attempted to arouse the people to the fraud from which they suffer, the private money creators—international bankers—arose in their might and used their controlled press, their bootlick politicians, their office boy bankers, their docile clergymen, and their power over the prosperity of America, to smash the drive for economic freedom. Thus far, they have succeeded.

33. How can Congress regain its privilege of issuing our money?

There is no need to regain what it has not the right to surrender. It still has that right, and can, and should immediately resume its exercise of this most important constitutional command.

Recapitulation

1. Money is any paper or coin imprinted or impressed by the Government seal to be used as a medium of exchange.

2. The Government and not private individuals should create this money.

3. The present and unconstitutional creators of money now exercise this right, thereby lending their created money at interest, or at a profit. In this way they get something for nothing.

4. This "something-for-nothing" becomes the farm or the home or the factory if the citizen-borrower cannot repay the loan.

Father Charles Coughlin

The Operation Of An Honest Money System

Restoration

1. What should the Citizens demand?

1. That Congress resume the exercise of its Sovereign Power—"to Coin Money and regulate the Value there-of; and of Foreign Coin".
2. That the exercise of the Sovereign Power be completely divorced from proper banking functions.
3. That banks be privately owned and restricted to their legitimate functions; i.e., Custodians and lenders of United States Legal Tender.

2. Why do we demand that Congress resume the exercise of its sovereign power?

To restore the highest function of our Government to those elected by the people. The social nature of man demands that the common denominator of all economic social functions be exercised by society as a whole or by those delegated and mandated by organized society.

3. What does sovereign power mean?

By sovereign power we mean a power belonging to all the people as a whole, without which the exercise of their National activities is impossible and without which the supreme jurisdiction, under God, over the citizens of a nation is likewise impossible.

4. Why do you say man is a social being?

Because he was created by Almighty God to live with his fellowmen. One man is a tailor, another a carpenter, another a fisherman and so forth. One man cannot live without his fellowmen and each citizen contributes some economic good not only for himself but for all citizens. The common denominator, or medium of trade, for all economic goods or services, is that one thing called money which belongs to no one individually but to all the citizens socially or collectively, insofar as it is coined and the volume regulated and put to use originally by the Government.

Opposing the Money Lenders

5. Why will Congress then be what was intended, the actual government of the United States?

> Because Congress, the legislative body created by the people, falls short of its ability to govern unless it possesses in itself this right to create and supply directly through its own proper appointees with specified duties the necessary medium of exchange to which no other function of the government is superior.

6. Why do you say that no other function of government is superior?

> Meyer Amschel Rothschild said: "Permit me to issue and control the money of a nation, and I care not who makes it laws." Precisely, if an individual or group of individuals control the issuance and regulation of money, the distribution system through which wealth is exchanged, it is possible for that individual or group of individuals to hamper trade, to constrict economic activity and to control the wealth of the nation itself.

7. Are self-chosen, non-elected, private individuals, corporations and groups now the de-facto government of the United States?

> Yes. The Federal Reserve Banks, private corporations whose entire stock is owned by private individuals, coin and regulate at least 95 per cent of the money used in the United States for the personal gain of stockholders. All the profits made by the activities of the Federal Reserve Banks accrue to the owners of these banks. Besides, inside advance knowledge of policies and their ultimate results, enable international bankers and international speculators to make enormous illicit profits, part of which they spend to protect their unmoral practices.

8. Are the Federal Reserve Banks identified with international bankers?

> Yes. The international bankers, or banks, are listed chiefly under the heads of the Federal Reserve Banks of the United States, the Bank of England, the Bank of France, the Reichsbank, the Bank of Italy, and central banks in practically every nation of the world. All these banks are owned by private individuals although they masquerade under titles which make them appear as if they were owned by the governments and peoples of these nations.

Father Charles Coughlin

9. How do international bankers operate for their own gain?

These private bankers owning, controlling and exercising for their own profits the money of all nations referred to, shuttle the gold and silver together with international loans, international acceptances and bank notes from country to country for the purpose of altering price levels to create gains for themselves and losses for the people. In this sense their patriotism is translated by the word "greed". Their country knows no boundaries and their flag is colorless.

10. Are the international bankers themselves unpatriotic and greedy men?

While some individual men may be honorable, their policies are unsound and unmoral and were conceived by persons by whom patriotism, democracy, justice and charity are not understood.

11. Has the local banker, with whom possibly you are acquainted, been responsible for these policies?

In most cases, no. Unfortunately, he has often been denied knowledge of the workings and the ultimate results of many policies dictated by a handful of international bankers. Consequently, he oftentimes has been their victim.

12. How can the Government of the United States be restored to honestly elected representatives of the people?

By completely divorcing the power to create money from proper banking functions and restricting to Congress alone the exercise of the sovereign power to issue (originate) and control the volume of money.

13. How can Congress resume the exercise of its constitutional mandate of the people to issue our money and control the volume thereof?

1. By nullifying the National Bank Act of 1863.

2. By nullifying the Federal Reserve Bank Act of 1913 and all intermediary and subsequent acts down to date.

3. By enacting legislation in harmony with the Constitution of the United States which mandates Congress "to coin money and regulate the value thereof; and of foreign coins".

Opposing the Money Lenders

This legislation must provide:

1. That a Congressional Board of Money, appointed by Congress, originate and pay into use interest-free money, bearing the seal of the United States Government and in sufficient volume to establish and maintain equitable price levels.

2. That a Congressional Board of Money handle exclusively all transactions in foreign exchange. Any exchange of dollars for the currencies of any other countries must be negotiated only through the Congressional Board of Money. All gold or silver (excepting token money) must be in the possession of the Congressional Board of Money and be used only for the settlement of international trade balances. The transfer of metals for the settlement of trade balances must not be at any fixed price per ounce. The price of foreign currencies must rise or fall with changes in price levels in other countries and the actual demand and supply of the various currencies in the foreign exchange market of the United States.

The present 2 billion, 800 million dollar secret stabilization fund should be removed from the jurisdiction of the Treasury Department and made the direct executive responsibility of the Congressional Board of Money.

The Secretary of the Treasury and his Department should be completely divorced from the Congressional Board of Money. The function of the Secretary of the Treasury is to collect and disburse tax payments. The Treasury Department should have nothing to do with recommendations or executions of orders relative to increasing or decreasing the supply of United States money in existence.

3. Banks should be privately owned, State-chartered corporations whose functions must be confined to acting as custodians and lenders of United States money which belongs to private citizens. The several government-owned lending agencies should be continued in existence until such time as the outstanding loans will have been liquidated or until such time as these loans are officially regarded as non-collectible.

Father Charles Coughlin

Scientific Principles To Be Observed

1. What is the purpose of a money system?

To make easy the exchanges of goods and services.

2. What, then, is the first requisite of an honest money system?

That general average price levels, as among the various classes of producers and distributors, be in proper proportion to each other, e. g. that farm commodities and other basic raw material prices be in proper proportion to finished manufactured goods prices.

3. Therefore, what would be the first duty of the Congressional Money Board?

They would acquire through scientific and accurate research the economic facts and statistics necessary to observe the movements of indices of price levels for the various classes of producers. These records and the manner of computation should be public.

4. What types of scientific economic data should be prepared and made public under the supervision and observation of the Congressional Board of Money?

1. Accurate indices of the prices at which basic raw commodities are exchanging for money.

2. Accurate indices of the cost of living (cost of the goods consumed in maintaining a reasonable standard) by a middle class family. e. g. A family of six living in a metropolitan area.

3. Complete and accurate figures on unemployment. These figures should be compiled from the various industries, by States and by ages. There are no accurate and complete figures on unemployment in this country today.

5. What is an index number?

An index number is a method adopted by statisticians and economic writers to exhibit the course of prices of a group of raw commodities or of commodities generally. The index number reduces initial prices to common terms. It establishes the variation of each price from its own starting point and then determines the average variation.

6. What are index numbers of raw material prices?

They are generally simple arithmetic computations representing the average prices at wholesale of a large number of raw commodities.

7. What do index numbers of the cost of living indicate?

They measure the relative cost of living (all of the items commonly used in living) as of different dates. They are generally expressed in terms of monetary units (dollars).

8. Why should an index number include a large number of commodities?

A sufficient number of commodities should be included to allow for particular demand and supply factors influencing individual commodities within the index. Price fixing of any single commodity is unsound.

9. What are average prices?

The mean prices of definite amounts, at specified times, of a large number of commodities.

10. Are changes in the supply and need of a large number of commodities the fundamental cause of changes in the price index of those commodities?

No. Average prices of a large number of commodities are influenced by arbitrary changes in the total number of dollars in existence.

11. What is the only test of the honesty of the money in use in a nation?

It is the amount of wealth (necessities of life) for which a given quantity of money may be exchanged. It is the constancy of its average exchangeability for goods and services that constitutes the acid test of the honest use of money.

12. Are there a number of index numbers in use in the United States today?

Yes, various Government agencies, at taxpayers' expense, and various private individuals and corporations have, for many years, prepared and kept up to date various index numbers. e. g. The index numbers compiled by the Bureau of Labor Statistics, the Federal Reserve Bank of New York, the Department of Commerce, various State and private universities, etc.

13. Have qualified persons accepted and used the various indices?

Yes, they are widely accepted and used but, strange to say, the Congress of the United States has never mandated the Federal Reserve Banks to keep in existence a volume of money required to establish and maintain specific average price levels.

14. Could qualified persons agree upon what particular indices should be observed and pass upon the accuracy of those indices?

Yes. That is a matter for qualified statisticians. Statisticians already maintain and observe a number of reliable and accepted indices.

15. What should determine how much money should be paid into use in the nation?

Observation of the movement of indices of price levels. For the ordinary citizen to get money, he gives up goods or his time and efforts in helping to produce goods. Money is the receipt for the wealth given up or the services rendered. A citizen holds money until he needs wealth. Thus, prices are a function of the volume of money in relation to the goods and services in the nation to be exchanged with money.

16. Why will observation of indices of price levels enable the Congressional Money Board to know when new issues of money should be added to the existing supply or when the existing supply should be reduced?

The reader will recall that the total volume of money in a nation represents the exchange value of the actual wealth which the owners of money are abstaining from possessing. Those who own money are owed wealth. Therefore, price levels are proportional to the quantity of money in existence divided by the wealth from which the owners of money (all of the people) are voluntarily abstaining from using.

Opposing the Money Lenders

Those who give up goods or services in exchange for money give up wealth before they receive money. As long as they hold money they are abstaining from the possession and use of wealth. The total amount of wealth from which the people will voluntarily abstain from owning or using, divided by the quantity of money in existence, determines the exchange value of money. As population increases and more wealth is produced, both because of a growing population and an increasing production per person, more money is necessary. The amount to be added can be determined only by observation of general average prices (index numbers).

17. Is the relation of prices of basic raw commodities to finished goods of primary importance in America?

Yes, because about fifty-five million persons are engaged, directly or indirectly, in the production of basic raw materials. If the prices they receive for new wealth are not in an honest ratio to the prices of the finished goods, producers not only cannot operate at a legitimate profit but they cannot be buyers of finished goods.

18. Then, is it necessary that equitable raw commodity prices be established and maintained?

Yes. The destructive effects of too low raw commodity prices have been experienced in this country in the agricultural depression which has existed from 1920 to date.

19. How can raw commodity prices be established and maintained in honest proportions to each other?

(a) By divorcing the domestic money supply from a gold or any other metal base.

(b) By abolishing fixed ratios for the exchange of dollars for the currencies of other countries.

(c) By establishing and maintaining an honest and adequate domestic volume of money.

20. Why would divorcing the domestic monetary quantity from gold or any other metal be necessary?

That movements of gold in or out of the country would no longer affect the amount of domestic money in use in the nation. Money issued (loaned) upon a metal base is the manipulators' stock in trade. Internationalists have only to remove part of the base to cause a collapse. For the workers and producers of the nation, the all important factor is the volume of money in relation to the goods and services to be exchanged with money. Producers earn money to buy the necessities of life—not gold. Only internationalists buy gold, not to eat or wear, but because gold is the base of the collapsible money structure, and its removal causes a collapse.

21. Why would abolition of fixed ratios in exchanging dollars or other currencies affect raw commodity prices?

Raw commodities such as wheat, cotton, oil, are for sale in all world markets. The amount of these commodities exported influences the price of these same commodities which are domestically used. Exports are possible only when foreigners can exchange their money for United States dollars at a favorable ratio. If foreigners must pay too many units of their currencies to obtain dollars they will not buy in the United States. Foreigners who buy our produce, owe us dollars. They must be able to obtain dollars to pay their bills without having to pay too many units of their own currency.

22. What does the Constitution say about the exchange of dollars for other foreign currencies?

The Constitution specifically mandates Congress to regulate the value of money and of foreign coins.

23. Does the word "regulate" mean stabilize?

Emphatically, No. The fact that internationalists have stabilized our currency enables them to play countries against each other. The very word "regulate" is a mandate to change the ratio at which dollars exchange for other currencies in accordance with well known scientific principles. That is in accordance with actual demand and supply and in accordance with changes in price levels within our own country or within the countries to which we are exporting.

24. Then, does it follow that the abolition of fixed ratios for the exchange of dollars for other currencies would benefit not only raw commodity producers but all classes?

Yes, it would enable us to enter the export markets with finished goods as well as with raw commodities.

Opposing the Money Lenders

25. Is the United States interested in exporting raw commodities and goods?

Yes, it is important that we export some of our basic raw commodities, such as wheat. And it is very desirable that our people, in turn, be able to buy certain luxury items in other countries.

26. Is it true that we now export only about 5% of our total production?

Speaking of production as a whole, that is true. But in certain single commodities we export a much larger percentage. Abolishing a fixed ratio and permitting exchange ratios to rise or fall in response to demand and supply and in accordance with changes in price levels in other parts of the world is the desirable situation. This would facilitate and expand enormously both domestic and foreign trade. Because foreign exchange is stabilized on a fixed gold basis we are suffering from artificial barriers. "Regulation", not "stabilization" is the key to the solution. Regulation of money demands a free gold and silver market.

27. What is a free gold or silver market?

One where the price of gold or silver is arrived at by the fundamental law of supply and demand, not one where the price is arrived at by government or central bank decree. (See Appendix II.)

28. How does an adequate volume of money affect raw material prices?

It increases mass purchasing power and, hence, affects the demand for food supplies, clothing, etc.

29. Should metal be used in settling international trade balances?

Yes, so long as other countries wish to use metals, the United States will meet their desires.

30. Why are trade balances specified?

Because no government should allow international speculators, arbitrarily, to transfer huge sums of money from one country to another merely for manipulative purposes. Foreign exchange should be allowed to take care of all legitimate balances of international trade. What is objected to and what is vicious is the arbitrary movements of enormous speculative balances between the various money centers of the world. These huge transfers are carried on merely for the purpose of tearing down price levels and playing countries against each other for the personal profits of the manipulators who control and operate on a fixed, stabilized gold standard.

31. If gold is used to settle international trade balances, should it have a fixed price?

No, the number of dollars per ounce of gold should correspond with the purchasing power of the number of units of other currencies. (Exchangeable for an ounce of gold). This will prevent internationalists playing one country against another.

32. May silver also be used to settle international trade balances?

Yes, if other nations wish to use silver. The United States has ample domestic sources to obtain silver and could enter the world markets as well.

33. Besides establishing raw material prices in proper proportion to finished goods, what other important relationship between money and wealth should be observed?

The whole price structure must be high enough to prevent those who have fixed income claims, such as bonds, from receiving too large a share of the new wealth produced each year. When the holders of fixed income can buy too much wealth with their dollars, the working classes suffer. No honest person wants to defraud people who have fixed incomes. As a whole, all people (excepting the few who benefit from manipulations) with fixed incomes would be tremendously benefited by an honest price structure, for they would then have assurance that their fixed claims could be received and exchanged for wealth. The properties into which their funds have been placed (as loans) would be in full production, and their incomes would be received regularly.

34. Is it proposed that the volume of money be changed to meet the demand of politicians?

Emphatically, no. The volume should be changed only in accordance with well defined scientific principles. Once equitable price levels have been established and full employment exists, the new additions to the money stream each year would be relatively small amounts of money.

Opposing the Money Lenders

35. *Why would the new additions of money each year be relatively small?*

After equitable general average price levels and full employment have been attained they must be kept stable.

New money can be paid into use only after genuine savings invested in producer goods and consumer goods in process have so increased the rate of production that additions to the money stream are necessary to maintain the established price levels.

36. *Would savings be unnecessary or be discouraged under an honest money system?*

Emphatically, no. Savings are absolutely necessary. The consumer wealth in process (being manufactured from raw commodities into finished goods) and the cost of all producer goods used in processing them must be financed out of savings. Genuine abstinence, to the full amount of the cost of goods in process and producer goods, is necessary, if honest price levels are to be maintained.

37. *Would it ever be necessary to cut down the volume of money?*

Yes, if the nation were to suffer from famine, flood or some force beyond the control of man so that actual wealth was destroyed. When there is less wealth to be exchanged, the volume of money must be cut down. Or again: If factories and machinery were destroyed through cyclones, fires, etc., it would be necessary to cut down the volume of money, because there would be less exchangeable wealth in existence.

38. *Why is it essential to have private investment (genuine savings) going into the construction of producer goods?*

1. Because producer goods, as they wear out and become obsolete, must be replaced.
2. About half of the workmen in this country are employed in the heavy construction industries. When legitimate private construction cannot proceed, these workmen are automatically forced to remain idle.

39. *Is there a reasonable need for more producer goods in a nation at any time?*

Yes, whenever reasonable want exists in the midst of plenty. For example, we need millions upon millions of new homes. But we permit an artificial constriction of our money system to keep workmen idle and the people in need of the very things which these work-men are able and ready to produce.

40. Is there any need for suffering want in the midst of plenty for a lack of money?

Absolutely no, because money is not wealth. There should be sufficient money injected into the money stream to enable the producers to produce, workers to work, and thereby create a supply to meet the reasonable demand at a profit for all engaged in any production or distribution.

41. If debts are contracted with cheap dollars when there is sufficient money in circulation, is it just and scientific to demand that these debts be paid back with dear dollars because there is less money in the money stream?

It is neither just nor scientific. If the price per hour for a laborer is $1.00 and, because there is not sufficient money in the money stream, the price for labor is reduced to 75 cents an hour, it would mean that, if that laborer had borrowed money previously when more money and high labor prices were in existence, he would be forced to repay his debt by one third more labor plus interest than he had contracted. There should be 100 pennies always in a dollar. By that is meant that the same amount of work performed by the laborer in 1928 should be sufficient in 1935 to meet his obligations.

42. Under our present dishonest system do bankers arbitrarily alter the price levels and thereby compel the borrower to pay back more (purchasing power) than he received?

Yes, bankers alter the price levels:

1. By increasing the volume of money without a previous proportional increase in the rate of production.

2. By decreasing the volume of money, thereby leaving goods and labor, either unsalable or salable only below the cost of production.

Opposing the Money Lenders

43. How would new money be paid into use?

When more money is needed, the Government would print it and pay it into use through the channels of legitimate government expenditures until the proper level of money would have been reached.

44. After honest price levels are established, would additions of money alter the price levels?

No. They would not decrease the value of previously outstanding money, because the new money would be added to existing amounts only after the rate of national production was increased. Thus, steady price levels would be maintained, despite increased production.

45. How would production be increased normally?

(a) By removing restrictions to production caused by artificial constriction of the medium of exchange.

(b) By an increase in population thereby increasing the demand.

(c) By citizens requiring more goods or services.

(d) By more citizens rising from below the standard of American living to the plane of the American standard of living and even beyond.

With our vast amount of raw wealth together with our army of scientists, engineers and skilled workmen it is not only possible but desirable that this plenty for all be produced and distributed.

46. Then, does not social justice advocate a redistribution of existing wealth?

No. Social justice demands the production of new wealth and its equitable distribution on the basis that there is plenty for all, if sufficient non-interest bearing money is paid into the money stream by the Government to establish equitable prices thereby enabling the reasonable demands of all citizens for goods and services to be supplied. Be it repeated that money is not wealth and that money should be our national servant, not our master.

Father Charles Coughlin

47. What is the chief racket of the private money creators today?

The chief racket of the private money creators today is their juggling the totality of outstanding money so as to juggle the price levels and thus manipulate the debt-paying power of money. The power of private individuals to juggle the price structure would be destroyed forever, if money were issued honestly and in accordance with well- known scientific principles.

48. Who would benefit by all new additions to the money stream?

As long as the nation is a going concern, it must have a money system. Therefore, the people should and would be the only power allowed to get the benefit of the original purchasing power of interest-free money as it is paid into the money stream. Private bankers now receive the "something for nothing" in the form of unearned interest on money which they lend into existence and which, arbitrarily, they can call out of existence. It is true the banker does not create money for his own spending, but he does create money for the purpose of enriching himself upon the unearned and fraudulent interest. Every time a private banker originates money to lend, he is levying indirect taxes upon all, and when he curtails the volume of money, he may legally confiscate property.

49. Is it reasonable to state that, if the government issues money, it will issue it in too large a volume?

No. Those empowered to issue money would have no incentive to over-issue money. They would not be the beneficiaries of the new purchasing power. Rather they would be held directly responsible for any unjust additions to the money stream. Full facts and figures regarding the volume of money in existence would be completely publicized in a manner intelligible to everyone who can read simple figures.

Opposing the Money Lenders

Effects Of A Dishonest Money System

What will happen if the present money system is continued and if the present policies endure?

1. Private individuals will coin money for their own personal gain.

2. Corporations organized for production, such as automobiles, steel and textiles, will be under the domination of the private money creators.

3. The government itself will be dominated by the money plutocrats.

4. The press, dependent upon advertising received from banker-dominated corporations and commercial houses, will continue to deceive the people.

5. The educational system will continue to ostracize the truths of economics from our schools.

6. An uninformed citizenry, forced to work either on the mortgaged-controlled farms or in the banker-controlled industries, will receive a less-than-living annual wage.

7. Through the international manipulation, of gold and money engineered by a small group of money creators living in each country, wars will continue to ensue.

8. The only prosperity which will come as a breathing spell will be that prosperity enjoyed as we prepare for war and fight the war.

9. The issue of non-productive bonds will continue to sap the profits of production through the process of taxation for the benefit of the creators of debt.

10. Those who now condemn loudly the danger of inflation in order to save the present money system are those who are introducing a greater flood of inflation than was ever experienced by any nation in the world.

11. The citizens, weighed down by the unbearable costs of war and depression, will be inclined to blame a democratic form of government and unwittingly relinquish the liberties already won for the bare

necessities of life, which the plutocrats will allow them only at the sacrifice of liberty.

12. Dictatorship, be it that of the communist, of the fascist or of the extreme socialist, will necessarily ensue.

13. Christianity, which teaches the principles of social justice and upon which is founded the sovereignty of the Government's right to coin and regulate the value of money, will be disavowed because Christianity will be blamed for putting war into the world instead of peace, poverty instead of prosperity and hatred instead of love.

14. The children of future generations shall be the scapegoats whom we are forcing to bear the sins of an unintelligent money system which, anticipating their birth, already has mortgaged their life's income.

15. Chaos in law, in government and in civilization eventually will result.

Advantages Of An Honest Money System

What will happen after an honest money system is established? An honest money system will help us:

1. To restore sovereignty over money to its rightful possessors, namely, the People, through Congress.

2. To insure the lastingness of democracy.

3. To rid Congress of servile politicians.

4. To make possible the attainment of a just, living annual wage for the worker and production at a profit for the farmer.

5. To prevent confiscation of honestly acquired property and savings of the people.

6. To eliminate from domination over the government the manipulators of money who oftentimes were the cause of war.

7. To insure lasting peace among nations whose governments will be able to legislate laws independent of the international money changers.

Opposing the Money Lenders

8. To make possible the real freedom of the press and the teaching of the truth in all schools, freed once and for all from the domination of money creators.

9. To insure independence for industry which today is dominated by finance.

10. To insure equitable credit for all manufacturers who are willing to pay a just, living wage for the production of a good product.

11. To enable every manufacturer to pay a just, living, annual wage free from the competition necessitated by the private control of money.

12. To eliminate the existence of non-productive bonds, such as Liberty Bonds, originated to borrow money for digging shell holes and killing soldiers.

13. To lessen the burden of taxation.

14. To re-establish banking on its original plane, namely, to make of it a function whereby the bankers will guard your money safely or will invest it to the best of their ability and divide the profits with you or will lend it to your fellow citizens for their welfare and the welfare of the social body.

15. To permit Christian virtue to be practised when want is destroyed in the midst of plenty.

16. To enable the youth of the land to marry: Young couples will look forward not into the shadows of depression but into the sunshine of prosperity.

Gottfried Feder

Gottfried Feder

The Breaking Of Interest Slavery

The party-line of the Left is that "Nazism" was the last resort of the capitalism. Indeed, the orthodox Marxist critique does not go beyond that. The libertarian "Right" indulges in something similar, as per Dr. Antony C. Sutton's *Wall Street and the Rise of Hitler*, for example. It is expedient to follow that line. However, expediency is not truth, expediency is not scholarship, and most of all expediency obscures the achievements that were wrought under the socio-economic and financial system of National Socialist Germany, as it does the pioneering achievements in regard to ecology (Anna Bramwell, *Blood & Spoil*, The Kensal Press, Buckinghamshire, 1985), public health, organic food, cancer research (Robert N. Proctor, *The Nazi War on Cancer*, Princeton University Press, New Jersey, 1999), and animal welfare. In broad respects the socio-economic and financial measures of National Socialist Germany were similar to those enacted around the same time by the iconic First Labour Government in New Zealand, and some other social-democratic governments elsewhere. Nor is it regarded as expedient for present day banking reformers, with some notable exceptions such as Dr. Ellen Brown and Dick Eastman, to objectively examine the banking reforms of Germany. Hence, a pioneer opponent of usury, or 'interest-slavery' and 'Mammonism', as he called it, Gottfried Feder, has been consigned to the memory hole, rather than being accorded the respect alongside other opponents of usury such as C. H. Douglas. This might have been different had Feder not, through supra-personal historical events, been involved in what became Hitler's NSDAP.

Feder had already presented his financial proposals in 1918 to the Soviet Bavarian republic and these had been rejected. As he notes in the autobiographical essay that follows, the breaking of 'interest-slavery' is alien to the orthodox socialist. One indeed looks unsuccessfully in Marx's *Das Kapital* and other socialist texts for an examination of and alternative to usury.

Gottfried Feder

Among the National Socialists, opposition to international capital figured prominently from the start, prior to the arrival of Hitler. The earliest programme of the German Workers' Party, in 1919, stated that the party was fighting "against usury... against all those who make high profits without any mental or physical work," the "drones" who "control and rule us with their money." It is notable that even then the party did not advocate "nationalisation" of industry but profit-sharing and symbiotic, organic unity between all classes other than "drones." (*Guidelines of the German Workers' Party*, January 5, 1919).

Hitler had been taught the distinction between productive capital and speculative capital from Feder who had been part of a political lecture series organised by the army. Hitler then understood that the dual nature of capital would have to be a primary factor addressed by any party for renewal. (Hitler, *Mein Kampf*, London, Hurst and Blackett, 1939, 180-181). The lecture had been entitled "The Abolition of Interest-Servitude." (Ibid., 183). Hitler wrote that a " truth of transcendental importance for the future of the German people" was that "the absolute separation of stock-exchange capital from the economic life of the nation would make it possible to oppose the process of internationalisation in German business without at the same time attacking capital as such... I had now found a way to one of the most essential pre-requisites for the founding of a new party." (Ibid.).

Gottfried Feder (1883-1941) was, like C H Douglas, an engineer. He studied at technical universities in Munich, Berlin and Zurich. In 1908 he established a construction company, and undertook several projects in Bulgaria. In 1917 he was drawn to the problems of banking and credit. In 1918 Feder wrote *The Manifesto for the Breaking of the financial Slavery to Interest*, directed at liberating all lands from "Mammonism." The work was sent to Kurt Eisner, head of the Bavarian Soviet Republic. However this elicited no response. As Feder was to point out, this is typical of Marxists, not least because striking at the root cause of class conflict, the banking system would disrupt the supposed "class struggle dialectic of history". In 1919 the Treaty of Versailles placed Germany firmly in the grip of international financial speculation. In September that year Feder founded the Federation for the Abolition of Interest Slavery. He joined with Anton Drexler, Karl Harrar and Dietrich Eckart in the German Workers Party (Deutsche Arbeiter Partei), which addressed the question of usury from the start.

Feder with Hitler and Anton Drexler wrote the 25 point programme of the NSDAP in 1920, the points on banking stating:

10. It must be the first duty of every citizen to perform physical or mental work. The activities of the individual must not clash with the general interest, but must proceed within the framework of the community and be for the general good.

We demand therefore:

11. The abolition of incomes unearned by work.

The breaking of the slavery of interest

Feder participated in the 1923 Munich Putsch but was only fined 50 marks. In 1924 he was elected to the Reichstag. In 1931 he was made chairman of the NSDAP economic council. When Hitler assumed government in 1933, Feder was made a State Secretary for economics but soon withdrew from government. He worked as a professor until his death in 1941. However, it would be an error to dismiss Feder's fundamental influence on Third Reich finance and economics, and claim that he was superseded by Big Business. The Feder plan was followed in the most fundamental ways.

The Third Reich

Hjalmar Schacht is instructive as to how the global banking nexus sought to co-opt the Nazi State—and how it failed. While researchers have focused on the first, they have neglected the implications of the latter. It is tempting to speculate as to whether Schacht was planted in the National Socialist regime to derail the more strident aspects of the NSDAP ideology on international capitalism. However, it is inaccurate to claim that Hitler betrayed the National Socialist fight against international capital, because the full economic program of the NSDAP was not fulfilled. There is usually going to be a difference in perspective as to what can be achieved when one is not in government. Schacht was obliged to work within National Socialist perimeters and could not help but achieve some remarkable results. That he ended up in a concentration camp because of his commitment to international capital is not mentioned by researchers such as Antony Sutton. Hitler had re-appointed Hjalmar Schacht as president of the Reichsbank in 1933, and in 1934 as minister of economics. Schacht wrote after the war:

> "National Socialist agitators led by Gottfried Feder had carried on a vicious campaign against private banking and against our entire currency system. Nationalisation of banks, abolition of bondage

to interest payments and introduction of state Giro 'Feder' money, those were the high-sounding phrases of a pressure group which aimed at the overthrow of our money and banking system. To keep this nonsense in check, [I] called a bankers' council, which made suggestions for tighter supervision and control over the banks. These suggestions were codified in the law of 1934... by increasing the powers of the bank supervisory authority. In the course of several discussions, I succeeded in dissuading Hitler from putting into practice the most foolish and dangerous of the ideas on banking and currency harboured by his party colleagues." (Hjalmar Schacht, *The Magic of Money* London, Oldbourne, 1967, 49)

What Schacht did introduce was the MEFO bill. Between 1934 and 1938 12,000,000 bills had been issued at 3,000,000 bills per year. MEFO bills were used specifically to transfer the exchange of goods. (Ibid., 117). However, once full employment had been achieved, Schacht wanted to return to orthodox finance. Hitler objected, and it was agreed that Schacht would continue as president of the Reichsbank until 1939, on the assurance that the MEFO issue would be halted when 12,000,000 bills had been reached. (Ibid., 114). After the war Schacht assured readers that fiat money such as the MEFO (Ibid., 116) like barter, should not become the norm for the world, despite the successes in Germany.

Likewise, Schacht opposed the autarchic aims of National Socialism. Schacht was, in short, ideologically inimical to the *raison d'etre* of National Socialism. Today he would be a zealous exponent of globalisation. He wrote after the war:

"Exaggerated autarchy is the greatest obstacle to a world-wide culture. It is only culture which can bring people closer to one another, and world trade is the most powerful carrier of culture. For this reason I was unable to support those who advocated the autarchistic seclusion of a hermitage as a solution to Germany's problems." (Ibid., 85).

Yet Schacht was also responsible during six years for re-establishing Germany's economy, and among the achievements which were in accord with National Socialism was the creation of bi-lateral trade agreements based on reciprocal credits. Schacht wrote of this:

"In September 1934 I introduced a new foreign trade programme which made use of offset accounts, and book entry credit...

My plan was to some extent a reversion to the primitive barter economy, only the technique was modern. The equivalent value of imported goods was credited to the foreign supplier in a German banking account, and vice versa foreign buyers of German goods could make payment by means of these accounts. No movement of money in Marks or foreign currency took place. All was done through credits and debits in a bank account. Thus no foreign exchange problem came into being." (Ibid., 85-86).

Schacht then hints at what would result in a clash of systems, and what might be contended was the real cause of the World War:

"Those interested in the exchange of goods came into conflict with those interested solely in money. There was soon a battle royal between the exporters who sold goods to Germany, and the creditors who wanted their interest. Both parties demanded to be given preference, but the decision always went in favour of foreign trade.

"I concluded special agreements with a number of states which were our principal sources of raw materials and foodstuffs. Anyone who wished to sell raw materials to Germany had to purchase German industrial products. Germany could pay for goods from abroad only by means of home-produced goods, and was thus able to trade only with countries prepared to participate in this bilateral programme. There were many such countries. The whole of South America, and the Balkans were glad to avail themselves of the idea, since it favoured their raw materials production. By the spring of 1938 there were no less than 25 such offset account agreements with foreign countries, so that more than one half of Germany's foreign trade was conducted by means of this system. This trade agreement system in which two countries—Germany and one foreign country—were always involved, has entered economic history under the name of 'bilateral' trading policy. (Ibid., 86).

"It created much ill-feeling in countries which were not part of the system. These were precisely those countries who were Germany's main competitors in world markets, and who had hitherto attempted to effect repayment of their loans by imposing special charges on their imports from Germany. The countries participating in bilateral trade were not amongst those which had granted Germany loans. They were primary producers or predominantly agrarian, and had hitherto scarcely been touched by industrialisation. They utilised the bilateral trading system to accelerate their own industrial development by means of machines and factory installations imported from Germany." (Ibid., 87).

However, Schacht was not even in favour of the permanence of this great alternative method of world trade that allowed for the peaceful development of backward economies. Imagine the difference in the world today had this system been allowed to live and grow? Schacht remained a member of the Banking cabal and he worried that

"The bilateral trading system kept the German balance of payments under control for many years, but it was not a satisfactory solution, nor was it a permanent one. It is true that it enabled Germany to preserve its industry and to feed its populace, but the system could not provide a surplus of foreign exchange. No more was ever imported than was exported. Import and export balanced out exactly in monetary terms. Thus this system achieved the very opposite of what I, in agreement with the foreign creditors, had deemed to be necessary." (Ibid., 87).

As if to emphasise that he had never intended to renege on the Banking cabal, Schacht lamented apologetically:

"Already at the time when I introduced the bilateral trading system I made it known that I regarded it as a most inadequate and unpleasant system, and expressed the hope that it would soon be replaced by an all-round, free, multilateral trading policy. In fact the system did have some considerable influence on the trading policies of Germany's competitors." (Ibid.).

It seems that Schacht had unleashed forces of economic justice and equity upon the world in spite of his intentions and it could only be stopped by war. Again: "For my part I would not say that the bilateral trading system, ranks among those of my measures which are worth copying." (Ibid., 89). Introducing barter in world trade seems to have been the source of great shame to Schacht.

Fiat money

Schacht criticises Hitler for having financed the war neither with taxation nor with the raising of loans. "Instead he chose to print banknotes," (Ibid., 98) which of course is anathema to a banker such

Opposing the Money Lenders

as Schacht, claiming the looming prospect of "inflation." True enough, the "inflation" did not occur because of the other state controls, but Schacht states that it did happen—in 1945. (Ibid., 143). At the end of the war the bills in circulation amounted to between 40,000,000 and 60,000,000 Marks. Schacht comments that it did not result in hyperinflation, and that the aim was to keep the level at that amount. (Ibid., 109). Might one conclude then that the fiat money – a dirty word nowadays among economists more than ever—that had been issued by the Third Reich had not been the cause of inflation, but rather the destruction of German production by the end of the war? At any rate it was not until 1948 that the Allied occupation attempted currency reform, based on the recommendations of U.S. treasury secretary Henry Morgenthau Jr., by a massive devaluation of the Mark. This is what had devastating consequences upon middle and working class Germans, and Schacht states that " malevolent intent was involved." (Ibid., 121). Fiat money has long been the great bugaboo among orthodox economists. Amusingly, Schacht spent two days during the Nuremberg proceedings trying to explain the MEFO bills, and when asked for a third time, gave up and refused. (Ibid., 118).

Bank of International Settlements reports show that up to the end of the war the Reich Government used a variety of methods of finance, including what Schacht had ridiculed as "state Giro 'Feder' money."

Another interesting point made by Schacht is that, contrary to the widespread assumption, German economic recovery was not based on war expenditure. Schacht even criticises Hitler with the assumption that he did not understand the requirements of war preparation. During 1935-1938 armaments expenditure was 14,000,000 RM. (Ibid., 101). Schacht assumes that this was due to Hitler's ignorance. The other alternative is that there was no long-term plan to wage a major war and prolonged aggression. There was no build up of raw materials and no real war economy until 1939.

In 1939 Schacht was replaced by Dr. Walther Funk, who had served in 1932 as deputy chairman of the NSDAP's economic council under the chairmanship of Feder. Working under the direction of Goering as head of the Four Year Plan, the replacement of Schacht by Funk seems to be an indication that a transitional phase had been completed and that the Government was well aware of Schacht's role as an agent for international capital. Otto D. Tolischus, writing from Berlin for *The New York Times*, as reported in Father Coughlin's *Social Justice*, commented:

"Dr. Schacht was ousted because he believed that Germany had reached the limit in debt-making and currency expansion, that any further expansion spelled danger to the economic system, for which he still considered himself responsible, and that the government would have to curtail its ambitions and confine itself to the nation's means...

"No authoritative explanation of the new financial policy is available so far, but judging from hints in the highest quarters, the policy is likely to proceed about as follows:

"Expand the currency circulation only for current exchange demands and not for special purposes.

"Open the capital market for private industry and make private industry finance many tasks hitherto financed by the State, either directly or by prices on public orders, which have enabled industry to finance the expansion of new Four-Year Plan factories out of accumulated profits and reserves.

"Create a non-interest bearing credit instrument with which the State, now having to share the capital market with private enterprise, will finance its own further orders in anticipation of increasing tax receipts from the resulting expansion of production.

"In one respect therefore, Herr Funk presumably will continue 'pre-financing' the State's orders as did Dr. Schacht, but whereas Dr. Schacht did it with bills, loans, delivery certificates and other credit instruments, all of which cost between 4½ and 5 per cent interest per year, Herr Funk proposes doing it with non-interest-eating instruments.

"How that is to be done is his secret, but the mere mention of interest-free credit instruments inevitably recalls the plan of Gottfried Feder which at one time fascinated Chancellor Hitler, but which Dr Schacht vetoed. ("The Abolition of Debt-Bonds is the Story Behind the Removal of Dr. Schacht," *Social Justice*, February 13, 1939, 11).

What had taken place was an ultimatum from the Reichsbank, which in January 1939 refused to grant the State any further credits. (Schacht, 117). This amounted to a mutiny by orthodox banking. On January 19 Schacht was removed as president of the Reichsbank, and his position

Opposing the Money Lenders

was assumed by economics minister Funk. Hitler issued an edict that obliged the Reichsbank to provide credit to the State.

Funk commented on Germanys' monetary policy a year later:

> "Turning from the external to the internal sector, the question, 'How is this war being financed in Germany?' is one in which the world shows a lively interest. The war is financed by work, for we are spending no money which has not been earned by our work. Bills based on labour – drawn by the Reich and discounted by the Reichsbank – are the basis of money…" (Funk, *The Economic Re-Organisation of Europe*, July 25, 1940).

Feder's ideas were being implemented. Even Schacht had to work within the milieu that Feder had created from his years of campaigning. The NSDAP broke the bondage of the international bank merchants, and this was being openly discussed around the world as the way of the future. Germany created an autarchic trading bloc both before and during the war, based on barter through a Reich clearing centre. Pegging national currencies to the Reichsmark resulted in immediate wage increases in the occupied states. The Bank of International Settlements Annual Report for 1940-1941 quoted finance spokesmen from Fascist Italy and the Third Reich:

> "The development of clearings in Europe has given rise to certain fears with regard to the future position of gold as an element in the monetary structure. It has since noted that Germany has been able to finance rearmament and war with very slight gold reserves and that the foreign trade of Germany and Italy has been carried on largely on a clearing basis. Hence the question is being asked whether a new monetary system is being developed which will altogether dispense with the services of gold."

In authoritative statements made on this subject in Germany and Italy a distinction is drawn between different functions of gold. The president of the German Reichsbank said in a speech on 26 July 1940 that "in any case in the future gold will play no role as a basis of European currencies, for a currency is not dependent upon its cover but on the value which is given to it by the state, i.e. by the economic order as regulated by the state." "It is," he added, "another matter whether gold should be regarded as a suitable medium for the settlement of debit balances between countries, but we shall never pursue a monetary policy which makes us any way dependent upon gold, for it is impossible to tie oneself to a medium the value of which one cannot determine oneself." (*The Bank of International Settlements Annual Report for 1940-1941*, 96).

Despite the minor role that Feder played in the Third Reich administration, his ideas, so far from being repudiated, laid the foundations of the National Socialist banking and economic policies. Is it not plausible that Feder, the theorist, would have made a poor bureaucrat? What has been determined, even from the statements of Schacht, who tried to circumvent Feder's ideas, was that (1) Debt-free state credit was used on a vast scale; (2) Foreign trade was based on barter, (3) Point 8 of Feder's original programme – "Joint stock corporations should use their profits to increase their productive capacity and nothing else. They should not be allowed to pay unprecedented dividends while at the same time assuming unprecedented debt" – was the basis on which big business was obliged to operate.

According to the Dividend Law of 1934, corporations were restricted on the amount of profits and dividends payable to shareholders to 6%. The remainder of profits had to be reinvested into the enterprise or used to buy Government bonds. (Richard Overy, *The Dictators*, London, Allen Lane, 2004, 438-439).

Opposing the Money Lenders

Inner History of the Abolition of Interest-Slavery

Fortunate is he who recognises the deep causes of things.—Virgil

"How did you really arrive at the abolition of interest-slavery?" is a question now often posed to me. I know not whether Columbus too was often asked: How did you really arrive at the discovery of America? The answer to such a question can and will turn out very differently, depending on the position that the questioner takes in regard to the matter and in regard to the person. In any case I want to try to give an answer that satisfies the questioner and – what I consider more important in such cases – satisfies in best conscience the one who was asked.

In recognising utterly important, perhaps the most important connections in the world's great questions, it is probably always a matter of a lightning-like intuition, of creative insight into hitherto obscure relationships, illumined by exciting prospects for the future. This birth of an idea, this sudden, clear cognisance of a truth, stands at the intersection of the inner and outer history of the idea.

The inner history is often obscure and hidden; it runs part of its course entirely in the subconscious. In all cases however evidence for the psychological development of an idea can be found by thorough investigation of inner experiences; concomitantly of course a certain mental orientation is the prerequisite for correctly evaluating the experiences of the soul.

This mental prerequisite however cannot be in any way based in the effect of specialised training, but lies much more generally in the correct instinct for certain relationships.

In my case a good sense of relative magnitude was perhaps the prerequisite for the final assembly of the, at first correctly sensed, and then scientifically verified, array of facts. And in my specialised work as an engineer this sure sense for the order of magnitude has always been for me more important and more dependable for results of calculations, or for the dimensioning of construction-components, than the results of the slide-rule and the table of logarithms, which of course produce numerically much more precise results, but do not give the correct "decimal point." It is upon the correct "decimal point" however, in other words upon the order of magnitude – whether ones, tens, hundreds, or thousands – that solutions to the most significant questions of economic policy depend, not upon the second, third, or fourth position in the number-series. The key consideration is not whether the German fixed-interest debt-burden amounts to 275 or 320 billion, and not whether the total capital of all German joint-stock companies amounts to 13.8 or 14.6 billion; the key consideration rather is that fixed-interest certificates demand an interest-payment of about 15 billion, whereas the total dividends of German industry in the best year amounted to only about one billion; thus it is a matter of the order of magnitude of 1:15, in regard to the proportion of the two most familiar forms of value-papers, fixed-interest assets and dividend-papers.

The impact of not-always-easy experiences in life and career upon the orientation of the soul—unlike the comfortable life based on income from mere possession of money, from interest and dividends—caused heightened attention to general economic and social affairs. As a young engineer and entrepreneur with too little capital for my wide-ranging entrepreneurial ambition, I soon became acquainted with the iron, pitiless grip of the impersonal Money-Power that first offers and gives the desired "credit," but then in every economic crisis proceeds exclusively in accord with the self-serving interests of capital. I then saw outside of Germany how the need of smaller states for credit was carefully nurtured and then the credit was "generously" given, for example the Disconto-Gesellschaft's 600 million given to Bulgaria in 1913-1914; but then what demoralising conditions of dependence of every kind also resulted from that. This is how the bridge was created, from narrow personal experience to comprehensive awareness of international relations. The awareness of strong, indivisible financial and moral interrelations was indeed present in the subconscious, but still not at all clear.

The Great War with its enormous impressions in the first years probably muddled the tracing of these financial problems, until the time when the gigantic financing of the World War through our war-bonds, and my uneasiness about the increasing indebtedness of the folk, fortified my attentiveness so much that I repeatedly protested even before banking professionals against the form of our much vaunted "sound debt" compared to the "floating debts" of France and England. Of course at the time I was more or less condescendingly smiled at, although it had to be conceded to me even back then that "of course with continuously increasing" indebtedness there could no longer be talk of a genuine "soundness" of the war-debt.

Opposing the Money Lenders

I would have regarded the indebtedness of the Reich through the certificate-press as enough in itself, without the obligation of further burdening the entire folk with high interest-payments, which, just like the debt itself, given the enormous figures coming into consideration, could never again be regarded as covered by the actual assets of the Reich, but could only ever be covered by the tax-potential of the entire folk. But for as long as a victorious end to the war left open the possibility of a complete or partial unloading of war-burdens, a thorough investigation of these affairs was neglected. As fate then fulfilled itself upon our poor German folk in those dark November days, then all of that experience and knowledge, conscious and unconscious, intuitive and rational, again awakened—and my now clearly recognised answer to the simple question, "What now?" was:

Abolition of Interest – Slavery !

In one night the first essay came into being, and already on 20 November 1918 I submitted to the government of the People's State of Bavaria [under Kurt Eisner] my basic principles and demands for the abolition of interest-slavery.

I emphasise that Socialist thought-processes in no way supported it.

Indeed, unlike the revolutionary slogan of liberty, equality, fraternity, the idea of the abolition of interest-slavery found very little understanding in the Marxist ministry. Not to mention that the capitalist-oriented press cloaked itself in icy silence.

With this emergence of the idea before the public, the idea begins its outer history, which then will answer the also frequently posed question: "What has happened thus far for the actualisation of the idea?"

Völkischer Beobachter, 1920, No. 72

Gottfried Feder

Programme of the Federation for the Abolition of Interest Slavery

Presented in Public Debate in Wagner Hall, Munich, 11 April 1921

The German Federation for the Abolition of Interest Slavery, hereinafter called "The Federation," demands the following:

1. We demand the nationwide discontinuation of interest payments, which is nothing more than robbery of the nation on behalf of global finance.

2. Specifically we demand revocation of the privilege given a certain private corporation, namely the Reichsbank, to print money anywhere in the country. This revocation should be accomplished through the nationalisation of the Reichsbank.

3. We demand nationalisation of all those banks that no longer perform their valid socioeconomic task of facilitating the circulation, movement and transfer of money. Those banks have ruthlessly taken command of our economic life. They are extorting tribute from the productive sector of our economy in the form of ever-increasing interest.

4. We demand adequate compensation for the devaluation of savings on behalf of small pensioners. The devaluation that resulted from the government's finance and tax policies has ruined everyone.

5. We demand specifically that the economic independence and future of Bavaria not be jeopardised by the assignment of our priceless natural resource, waterpower, to private finance capital.

6. We demand that the State undertake the development of water resources by utilising our own labour resources. The State should create the necessary monetary instruments through its own financial authority. These instruments will be covered by income from the power plants that are built.

7. We demand that the State use its national assets and taxing power for productive undertakings, not to provide necessary collateral for borrowing money.

Opposing the Money Lenders

8. We demand restrictions on the raising of capital by corporations. Joint stock corporations should use their profits to increase their productive capacity and nothing else. They should not be allowed to pay unprecedented dividends while at the same time assuming unprecedented debt. These massive amounts of new (borrowed) money represent more debt, demanding additional interest that can only lead to increased inflation.

9. The Federation rejects the imputation that its demands are "utopian" and "designed to spread unrest among the people."

The recovery of our national economy can be achieved only by discontinuing national debt service, is vitally important for everyone. Therefore, it is not "utopian."

Whatever public unrest exists is created by the opponents of economic recovery and by no one else. It is true that individual selfish interests will be harmed here and there, but discontinuation of interest payments is a necessary act that can no more be avoided than can a life-saving operation be avoided on account of the associated discomfort.

The Federation insists that the national economic crisis demands a solution!

The havoc wreaked by our financial policies is affecting the entire nation!

These failed policies aggravate all our social problems.

At present, our government cannot satisfy the private need for credit.

An effective programme would entail a complete abolition of interest, for which there is historical precedent.

At present, interest rates are left to the unrestricted demand of the lenders.

A solution to the present crisis can be found only by requiring the lender to share risk as well as profit. The lender should not receive a blanket guarantee on investment plus other ever-increasing charges plus the constant unearned growth of wealth through fixed interest.

Gottfried Feder

The Federation proposes the liberation of all Western nations from their stupendous indebtedness. The abolition of interest slavery is the necessary prerequisite for the solution of every country's crisis, not just Germany's crisis. We have proposed a plan to end the titanic struggle now raging between Labour and Capital in favour of the freedom to work and produce. Our plan shows how to accomplish this without undermining the acquisition of wealth through individual effort, industriousness and intellectual achievement.

Only by abolishing interest slavery can Germany achieve reconciliation in a nation torn by class conflict. It can be achieved only by putting an end to the unearned income that is derived from the possession of money.

Our greatest social task is the abolition of interest slavery. This responsibility to abolish interest slavery towers above all other issues of the day.

It is the only solution to the greatest problem of our time.

The abolition of interest slavery will deliver us from global Capitalist domination. It will accomplish this while avoiding both Communist destruction of the human spirit and Capitalist degradation of labour.

The abolition of interest slavery opens the way to a truly social economy, by liberating us from the overwhelming domination of money.

It opens the way to a state based on creative work and genuine accomplishment.

Conclusion

It is hoped that this collection of essays on the most vital issue, now as ever, has cogently explained what is often presented as a complex matter. This is a titanic struggle that has taken place through the ages, often hidden, while wars, revolutions , poverty, and the rise and fall of entire civilisations, swirl around generation after generation of hapless folk, dying for causes, states, religions and ideologies while the power and the profits of the money-brokers compound by leaps and bounds as much as their usury.

We have in addition to the essays also brought something of the characters and struggles of some of the great advocates of liberation from Mammonism. They fought a great fight, sacrificed, and are now largely forgotten or vilified. Yet this is the fight that is relegated by historians and economists to dry theories, analyses of balance sheets and descriptions of a myriad of economic terms.

Meanwhile, those who claim to be working to save what remains of Civilisation are often preoccupied with debates about matters that should long have become passé. One still sees, when on the rare occasion the question of usury is raised, sterile debates on the efficacy of returning to a gold or a silver standard. The problems were long ago identified as were the solutions. This seems to have been forgotten by those who are fixated on secondary issues at best, and where political action exists it is of the character of a knee-jerk reaction.

Hopefully in this volume one finds the problems identified, and the solutions explained in a manner that presents more than an economic theory, but rather a fighting creed.

Further reading from Black House Publishing.

Kerry Bolton, *The Banking Swindle*

Stephen Mitford Goodson, *A History of Central Banking and the Enslavement of Mankind*

Stephen Mitford Goodson, *Inside the South African Reserve Bank – Its Origins and Secrets Exposed*

Gottfried Feder, *Manifesto for the Breaking of Interest-Slavery*

Gottfried Feder, *The German State on a National and Socialist Foundation*

Gottfried Feder, *The Programme of the NSDAP*

www.ingramcontent.com/pod-product-compliance
Lightning Source LLC
Chambersburg PA
CBHW050801160426
43192CB00010B/1600